A Handbook for

Deterring Plagiarism

in Higher Education

Jude Carroll

Oxford Centre for Staff and Learning Development

© Oxford Centre for Staff and Learning Development 2002

Published by
THE OXFORD CENTRE FOR STAFF AND LEARNING DEVELOPMENT
Oxford Brookes University
Headington
Oxford
OX3 0BP

A Handbook for Deterring Plagiarism in Higher Education
ISBN 1-873576 56 0

British Library Cataloguing-in-Publication Data.
A catalogue record for this book is available from the British Library.

Designed and typeset in Palatino and Helvetica by
Meg Richardson (megrichardson@btconnect.com).

Printed in Great Britain by
Technique Studios Limited
www.techniquestudios.com

Printed on paper produced from sustainable forests.

Contents

Acknowledgements

Many people have directly and indirectly contributed to my ideas and understanding of plagiarism. Some of their contributions can be recognised in the conventional way by citation and bibliography and I have tried to do this in the text itself. Here, I can thank a few people directly and admit I can no longer remember exactly where an idea, insight or new activity came from. Many of the suggestions appear frequently in guides like this one – perhaps that makes them common knowledge? Many just seem like common sense but perhaps someone somewhere claimed this idea and I ought to cite it. I can no longer remember if the example of an essay that mentions the Princess of Wales as if she was alive (a trigger for further investigation of students copying previous work, surely) is one I thought up or one I encountered. In this matter, I resemble students who often feel a similar sense of confusion when knowledge now feels a part of oneself. I have learned from chats at conferences, corridor conversations with friends, or emails passing on student quotes like, "I had a student this week who admitted the plagiarism but said he wasn't to blame because the person he copied from didn't tell him it was plagiarised..." If I have passed off someone else's work as my own in this Handbook, I apologise and would welcome this being drawn to my attention.

Some help is easy to acknowledge because it is still directly linked in my mind to the helper: Jon Appleton for sharing his skill at developing and clarifying policy matters and for the ideas in Chapter 8; Hazel Peperell who knows more about electronic detection than I ever will and who regularly demonstrates the capacity for creative detective work; Gill Chester who asked me to begin writing in this area as part of the JISC project and then became a generous networker; Paul Richardson, Margaret Price and Lynne Errey who commented on the text and suggested changes; Clare Collinson, Meg Richardson and Elizabeth Smith who turned a scruffy manuscript into a book; and my colleagues in the Oxford Centre for Staff and Learning Development who tolerated all the traumas of authorship.

Above all, I thank the hundreds of colleagues, lecturers, students and participants at workshops I have run over several years and in several countries. Their reactions and feedback have taught me what works for staff and students and what activities are important if we are serious about doing something about plagiarism.

Preface

Suggestions on using this book and a few words of advice

This handbook collects together the ideas, activities, research findings and comments I have accumulated over several years of working with academic colleagues on the issue of deterring plagiarism. I have used the activities described in workshops and conference presentations. I have tried them out on students, checked them out with colleagues and include them here in the hope they will serve as a resource and shortcut to action for busy colleagues. If this ties in with your reasons for reading this book, I suggest you start by reading the first chapter to become familiar with the topic then dip in and out of other chapters as and when they seem relevant.

I also intended this handbook to alert readers to issues they might not have considered. If you are interested in taking a holistic approach to deterring and detecting plagiarism, I suggest you explore most if not all the book. However, as the handbook's focus is on taking action rather than a literature review aimed at reflection, the following advice might be useful:

Start small, start simply

It is possible to do something about plagiarism by starting anywhere in this handbook and by adopting a single action (at least as a start). Tackling plagiarism need not overwhelm other important considerations for teachers. An experienced colleague said recently, 'It [plagiarism] needs putting in proportion without in any way diminishing its importance. Once you embed various practices like using plagiarism-resistant assessments and once you work on students' attitudes like knowing what it is and how seriously we view it, it does not have to be a centre stage issue all the time'. As you read, keep the focus on taking the first step rather than mapping the whole journey. However, I have noticed that where institutions and individuals combine a range of actions together and think strategically about what they are trying to achieve, the effect is amplified.

Be realistic

You will find some comments and suggestions in this handbook that are irrelevant given your own circumstances and interests. For example, I often suggest in workshops that there is merit in checking authenticity (that is, trying to discover whether the student who submitted a piece of work is the real author) by using a viva or observing the creation of a piece of writing. Those with classes of 250 throw their hands up in horror, crying, 'Impossible!' If you have a similar reaction to any suggestion, ignore that suggestion. There are probably many other ways which will have an equal or even larger deterrent effect.

You also need to be realistic about how much time you are willing to devote to deterring plagiarism. Some aspects are very time consuming such as collecting evidence to support an accusation (it takes hours or days), teaching the skills students need to avoid it (it takes days or weeks), or embedding good practice within an institution (it takes years). You probably cannot achieve those long-term things alone but will need to involve colleagues, the management, or even outside experts. Other actions are relatively straightforward but nevertheless take time to plan, carry through and evaluate. One of the purposes of creating a handbook is to alert you to aspects that, whilst not addressed at the moment, might be adopted later, leading eventually to a comprehensive and holistic approach.

Be flexible, stay ready to change your approach

As institutions get better at addressing the current worries, new ones will probably arise. Electronic detection schemes are being developed and academic rules and requirements change regularly. Research into plagiarism is fairly sparse at the moment but is growing apace. All these factors mean that, though I have tried to be as accurate and timely as I could in putting this handbook together, some of the information will be overtaken by events and new technologies on the day of publication. Equally, you may find that what works with one group of students or one problem, won't work with the next. Hopefully, there will be sufficient variety in what is suggested under each heading in this handbook to trigger rethinking and review.

Check your own beliefs and motivation

Deterring and detecting plagiarism usually boils down to one person taking or not taking action. Sometimes the reasons for avoiding action are linked to the issues already mentioned such as not knowing where to start or being worried about the amount of time required. However, I have found it far more often to be linked to a lecturer's beliefs and personal concerns: 'If I find plagiarism, will I look bad compared to my colleagues?' 'If I spend my time on this, when will I do research?' 'If I make an accusation, will it be handled with the seriousness I would wish?' I have never found addressing these worries directly leaves the other person reassured. Instead, I have decided to write this handbook in the hope that anyone with a reason for not acting might discover for themselves a range of counter-reasons for acting. I have stressed the help and support all of us will need to be effective. Institutions, colleagues and students must all play their part if we are to halt or even reverse the growing number of students who try to gain credit for work they have not done. This is even more important in catching and punishing the small but growing number who seek academic qualifications through fraud rather than effort. I think it is worth doing something about this and I hope, once you have used this handbook in whatever way seems best for you, you will, too.

Real fear or media hype?

The number of reported cases of plagiarism in UK higher education institutions continues to be very low, often amounting to only a few per year in large universities. Most academics I talk to feel this is an underestimate and many of the statistics cited at the beginning of the next chapter confirm the view. However, press interest, startling headlines and discussions amongst worried academics often make it seem as if plagiarism constitutes a systematic and wholesale assault on the assessment system in HE. What's more worrying is the growing climate of unease and distrust, making academics feel less confident that they are accrediting student effort. Students, too, might be affected by the growing emphasis on preventing and catching cheaters. It could be that students who do not cheat – apparently the large majority – feel it is becoming harder to continue not to do so. Also, studies of student motivation for cheating (See Chapter 1) reveal other aspects that could mitigate against obeying the rules such as the view that some teachers don't care or that students are being asked to do meaningless things. These issues are addressed in a range of ways throughout this handbook.

Knowing institutional policies

An individual student or academic operates within an institutional framework of regulations and procedures which, in turn, function in accordance with national and even international guidelines and legal frameworks. Chapter 8 on policies and procedures might help inform your practice but becoming familiar with your own university's policies certainly will. Often, this does not happen. Walker (1998) found widespread ignorance:

… academic staff appear not to be fully aware of what institutional policies exist regarding student plagiarism … as a result, staff may be dealing with cases in a random, haphazard manner (p.99).

This is a finding my own experience confirms. Requirements about operating within frameworks and following guidelines are becoming ever stronger, as is the frustration that can be felt when decisions are reached on the grounds of regulation rather than the merits of the case.

Jude Carroll

Reviewing the issues

1

What is plagiarism?

> ### Think about:
>
> Are you, your colleagues and your students clear about the distinction between:
>
> - cheating and plagiarism?
>
> - plagiarism and poor academic practice?
>
> - collaboration and collusion?

Defining plagiarism

Any effort to deter plagiarism usually starts with seeking a definition that everyone can accept. Here's one used in many institutions:

> Plagiarism is passing off someone else's work, whether intentionally or unintentionally, as your own for your own benefit.

Each part of the definition merits further clarification:

- **passing off** acknowledges the distinction between the private and public work – it is only plagiarism when you go public. Passing off also implies either giving a false impression (which might happen inadvertently) or trying to trick someone, which is probably a deliberate act. Many definitions emphasise this point, sometimes using language which addresses the student directly, as in this example from McNaughton (1995):

  > 'Plagiarism' can be defined as the attempt to gain advantage for yourself – academic advantage, financial advantage, professional advantage, advantage of publicity – by trying to fool someone, such as a teacher, an editor, an employer, or a reader, into thinking that you wrote something, thought something, [constructed something] or discovered something which, in actual fact, someone else wrote, thought, [constructed] or discovered.

Plagiarism is sometimes defined, aphoristically, as 'literary theft'. [The information in brackets could be added to further widen the scope beyond writing.]

- **someone else's work** – the definition mentions someone else's work, not just their words. Many definitions focus too narrowly on text, whereas plagiarism is about the student not doing the work. This is a useful distinction because it goes beyond what is covered by copyright to include such things as constructions, images, organisational structures, compositions, and ideas. Academics may welcome here a slight digression into the realms of 'autoplagiarism' which may occur when you quote yourself without attribution, as the copyright to previously published work often belongs to your publisher. Evans (2000) reminds us that the phrase, 'even if I do say so myself' may need to finish with a citation.

- **intentionally or unintentionally** is a useful phrase to remind the student that regardless of why it happened, their actions constitute plagiarism. Intention may have an impact on what happens once plagiarism is confirmed (see Chapter 7 on fair punishments and procedures).

- **as your own** – this phrase carries a complex message as it asserts individual ownership of ideas, work and words. It also assumes that whoever first publicly 'claimed' the idea is the 'owner'. Students find this concept difficult as they rightly point out that everyone builds on and depends upon others' ideas. They also see it as potentially fraught with danger, as they cannot be expected to search high and low for prior claims for ideas they see themselves as generating. Unless students themselves bring up the issue, it may be more useful to discuss these more complex aspects with students studying at postgraduate level or with those who are experienced at higher education assignments. However, the issue is also a perfect lead into discussing why citing others strengthens their writing and gets better marks.

- **for your own benefit** usually means a mark or grade but it might include a promotion, stronger bid for funds, or enhanced professional reputation.

All aspects of the definition are important for clarifying the distinction between collaboration and collusion, too. **Collaboration** describes the work of learning and is highly valued by teachers and learners. As soon as a student passes off work done jointly as if it had been done individually or passes off work where no student effort was involved, perhaps by copying, he or she is giving a false impression to the

In my own subject area of dance … I can recall two instances when an investigation of plagiarism in student practical submissions has been necessary. On one occasion, an assessor viewed her own choreography …presented without acknowledgement. On another, assessors recognised material from a professional work…

Stevens (2002)

assessor, either intentionally or unintentionally. That's **collusion**. Many students complain that this distinction is not made clear to them or that they are not given clear guidance on how to submit evidence of their individual effort and learning. The distinction becomes especially problematic when a cohort is set a task with a single correct answer or resulting in a similar artefact. This issue is addressed in Chapter 2 on course design and in Chapter 4 on informing students.

Ensuring students understand what plagiarism is

Cheating is seeking to gain unfair advantage or breaking a regulation; plagiarism is one form of cheating. Students often reverse this relationship, using the word 'plagiarism' to describe all academic dishonesty, so time spent clarifying definitions is usually time well spent. They are often also unclear about the difference between rules governing plagiarism and those covering copyright. Copyright, in general, protects people's words; plagiarism extends this coverage to ideas, structures and work. Sometimes these distinctions are difficult for both staff and students. This handbook offers several exercises in later chapters designed to engage staff and students in creating and confirming assumptions about plagiarism.

Consensus with colleagues

The definition of what constitutes plagiarism will vary depending on:

- the rules of particular disciplines (biologists, for example, see this very differently from historians);

- the context (citation requirements in essays, oral presentations, reflective journals and exams will all vary);

- the level at which something can be treated as common knowledge (a first–year undergraduate, for example, may be required to cite the most widely read and fundamental works in the discipline; a masters–level student who has, to some extent, joined the discipline and begun using the discourse of the discipline, may be able to refer without citing);

- the institutional frameworks and regulations (see Chapter 8); and

- professional requirements (if any) for example, some professions wish to be informed of all academic misconduct with a view to preventing unsuitable applicants from being licensed; this means that actions which breach academic conventions but which are not fraudulent may have a disproportionate effect on those who are found guilty (see also page 75).

[Student uncertainty] can create anxiety and fear of inadvertant plagiarism for some students. For example, it was felt by a number of first years that you could get accused and punished for plagiarising an idea they thought was their own but had in fact already been thought of and written in a book.

Freewood (2001, p. 2)

It therefore follows that definitions of plagiarism and collusion are best agreed locally through discussion and consensus. One word of warning: it is probably not helpful to share the levels of complexity described in the above points with students. Students already find this area dangerously ambiguous and feel disempowered by having to operate in contested situations where the consequences of getting it wrong might be severe. However, it is useful to share the results of deliberations between academic colleagues with your students.

See page 46, amongst others, for suggestions on how you might use activities to engage students and colleagues in these matters.

How widespread is plagiarism in higher education?

> ### Think about:
>
> - what is your experience with student plagiarism?
>
> - what have you encountered or heard colleagues talking about?
>
> - what about your own student days – did you cut corners, take shortcuts, make up citations or collude with fellow students?
>
> - how seriously do you view the problem?

In 1995, the first major review of undergraduate cheating in the UK was published (Franklyn-Stokes and Newstead, 1995) with the useful subtitle 'who does what and why?' It opened the discussion of cheating in the UK and built on a large body of literature from the USA which has since grown to dominate the field as the resources in pages 89–91 demonstrate. The authors concluded that the British experience in the mid-1990s was similar to that reported in other countries, with more than 60% of students in their study reporting 'behaviours such as copying each other's work, plagiarism and altering and inventing research data' (p. 159). Their findings showed that 72% of students interviewed admitted to copying coursework, 66% paraphrased without acknowledgement, and 54% fabricated references. Yet despite this high level of activity, a search of the available literature 'failed to reveal a single paper concerning any aspect of cheating behaviour in the UK', a finding they describe as 'curious'. Subsequent studies in the UK have been keen to assert that this was not analogous to Phillip Larkin's claim that sex was discovered in 1963.

Some plagiarism statistics

- Fly et al (1997) found that 15% of a group of US psychology students claimed that they had cheated in one way or another.

- 29% of a group of US medical students surveyed by Coverdale and Henning (2000) admitted falsifying references and 17% had submitted material copied from previous year's papers.

- Walker (1998) cites a survey of 200 US business students which revealed that 80% frequently cheated and 19% had specifically committed plagiarism. He went on to say that British research studies had produced similar findings.

- Bull and Collins (2001) surveyed 321 UK academics and found that 70% believed that plagiarism was a 'significant problem in academic institutions' and 50% believed the problem had increased in recent years.

- A survey of teachers of computing found that students plagiarised 'some, most or all of the time' in initial courses. When the findings for all courses were combined, accusations modally involved less than 20% of students (Culwin et al, 2001).

In private conversations most academics describe findings such as those above as 'only the tip of the iceberg'. However, such assertions and the published statistics are both hard to evaluate. Most studies do not provide the context for their statistics. When students confess to cheating, are they admitting to:

- a one-off event or serial plagiarism?

- copying a few lines of text or a significant portion of a work?

- cheating in a relatively minor piece of work or in one that will determine a degree classification such as a dissertation? or

- a misuse of academic conventions for citation or wholesale downloading of unaltered text off the Web?

In fact, it is not necessary to determine exactly how big a problem plagiarism is to consider it a problem worth tackling. By its nature, plagiarism threatens the value and integrity of what is being taught. It

A THES article on plagiarism in January, 2002 produced the following response:

"I have just finished marking 77 second year degree essays, and found 15 to have been lifted straight from the net without quoting the appropriate references. To cap it all, these essays were submitted by students on a computer ethics module!"

If approximately 20% of students resort to cheating having studied ethics and law and intellectual property rights, what does it say about the level of plagiarism and cheating on other courses? The academic in question is now thinking of doing some serious research on the subject ...

THES 15 January 2002, p. 11

threatens students' engagement with learning and, unless addressed, could undermine the worth of the awards students earn.

Is it the Web?

Most cases of plagiarism arise from misuse of print–based resources. A study in 2001 (Chester, 2001) confirms what I hear repeatedly from academics: unreferenced copying from books, journals, course notes and other students is more common than straight copying from the Web. IT-based courses usually are the exception – students on these courses have both the skills and the opportunities for using electronic material, both appropriately as resources and inappropriately as plagiarism. However, academics who affirm the predominance of print-based plagiarism also note that students' skills and access to electronic media grow month on month, leading to concern that those who currently do *not* cheat face growing opportunities and temptations to do so. Mostly, those growing temptations arise from electronic rather than print-based opportunities. When academics worry about plagiarism arising from fraud rather than misunderstanding, most of the worries are about electronic resources.

A growing number of so-called 'paper mills' offer essays for sale and student newspapers alert students to their existence. Startled academics visiting the sites, find essays and research papers, both for sale and for free, catalogued by topic and by discipline. One free US site (www.schoolsucks.com) received 40,000 hits per day in 1998 (Boehm, 1998). Although this particular site is aimed at secondary-level students, its popularity indicates an approach to study and a level of familiarity that may bode ill for the future college work of its 'customers'.

British sites are now appearing, too, and although many offer the same essays as their US counterparts, others tailor their output to the UK market or to particular disciplines such as law in the example opposite Some sites offer so-called study help and guidance on how best to modify and adapt essays to escape detection. I have often found that setting up a few sites and encouraging colleagues to browse what is on offer focuses their attention on issues such as course design and the place of essays in assessment. It also helps to balance unrealistic fears as lecturers find that most are of very dubious quality and overwhelmingly aimed at the American High School market. For suggestions on other ways to use cheat sites, see page 58 below; the resources pages suggest urls to start your own exploration if you are unfamiliar with such sites.

Cheat sites and paper mills

Today's student has a choice of scholarly and pseudo-scholarly resources such as Web sites that either give away or sell complete research papers on any topic required. Beware the assumption that because the sites are predominantly American, the market does not apply in the United Kingdom. There are reasons that those sites have international order forms. If you are looking for a local flavour, try Law Essays Bank, Finchley Law Tutors [on http://www.knowledge.co.uk/lawessays/index.htm], selling essays for a minimum £30 fee.

Evans, J (2000) The New Plagiarism in Higher Education on http://www.warwick.ac.uk/ETS/interactions/vol4no2/evans.html

Since 1995, the number of Web pages available has grown by tens of thousands of pages per day and the rate is accelerating. Many are suitable for cut-and-paste plagiarism and/or wholesale downloading of text. Resulting documents are easily reformatted to look like, and with minor tweaking, read like the student's own work.

Students' understanding of acceptable ways to use Web-based information has not kept pace with the exponential growth of the Web. Gajadhar (1998) describes commonly held student views such as the belief that material on the Web is free for anyone to use, or the view that changing a few words makes a downloaded text 'my own work' as Jenifer implies in the quote below. Gajadhar asked students to classify scenarios involving the Web as either plagiarism or acceptable and found their responses divided almost exactly 50/50, demonstrating student confusion.

Mirow and Shore (1997) argue that digitalising text per se, regardless of its origins, changes the relationship between author and reader and makes plagiarism more likely. They argue that moveable type made authors see their work as valuable and therefore worth defending from the wider readership's use, thus triggering copyright laws. However, digitalising text means anyone can use it, manipulate it and seem to 'own' it so that students become 'word brokers'. Once they detach blocks of texts from their original authors (often losing the attribution information through 'inattentive research practices' (p. 42), they then treat the captured blocks as their own.

From the horse's mouth

An American student named Enid Carlson set up a Web page in the USA where students could upload their own essays and download those of previous contributors at no cost. Enid's site received over 1 million hits before her university threatened her with expulsion. She removed it prompting hundreds of comments like those below from disappointed users.

> Sometimes when you read something good that someone else wrote, it will inspire you to write a good paper yourself. I always looked up more information and changed it around a little. It's not like I wasn't doing any work or using this to cheat, it was a helper.
> jenifer

> I'd like to say that I am one of those cheating students, and I have copied some of your work, or plaguirsed if you will. Plagurism existed before the net. Plagurism will always exist and taking down one site wont stop me at all.
> Morphius

> I support people who operate cheating sites. The cost of college is skyrocketing. Fat cat college professors exist off my tuition money but are too terribly busy to teach the classes that they complain about students cheating in.
> Ryan Watson

> I would just like to express how much of a shame it is that you got shut down. I have always used your sight to start off my reports. Honestly I am not the best of writters and I dont always know where to start. I used your essays as a unblocker for my brain, And not all the time but usually it would work great. I am not going to say its some kinda marvilous cure for writters block, its just a great assisten
> Matt

(All the above and more were found in 2000 on http://elee.calpoly.edu/~ercarlson/papers.htm)

Plagiarism puts Monash VC out of job

---

*Vice Chancellor Robinson left his post in a leading Australian University "by mutual agreement" when the THES Whistleblowers column reported two cases of plagiarism in the late 1970s and early 1980s then, two weeks later, reported that the selection panel who had appointed him six years earlier was not aware of "his past record". His departure was seen as being "in the best interest of the University".
A university spokesperson said that future candidates would probably not be asked if they were plagiarists.*

THES, 19 July 2002

This is not a new phenomenon, nor is it unique to students. The literature on plagiarism frequently cites high profile cases of academics charging others with using work without correctly attributing it. The difference now is that, as Evans (2000) argues, when students went to the library, found a book, copied the relevant words and transcribed them to their own coursework, at least some learning may have resulted. The Internet allows (in some cases) the opportunity to meet course requirements and bypass any thinking at all.

Digitalising text also offers more convenient opportunities for collusion, creating informal essay banks from last year's work, swapping work between institutions and cobbling together a piece of work from material gathered from several friends. However, to repeat the point made earlier, both the literature and academics I meet continue to cite print sources as being much more of a problem, as they see the majority of plagiarism originating there.

An enterprising approach to cheating

A *Guardian* newspaper article by L. Major (*Guardian*, 8 January 2002, p. 9), about Elizabeth Hall Associates, 'a retired lecturer selling essays to students over the Internet', quotes an email from her which said,

> I would be very happy to write a series of essays for you, and complete the final year of your degree. I am sending to you my charges ... I offer you absolute confidentiality and in no circumstances would I reveal to anyone our contract. You need not worry that the authorities would discover the work is not your own. In some cases I can, if felt necessary [sic] that the work I am writing might seem as above the grade that could be attained by the student, actually build in material which I know is incorrect, so that the grade does not cause any alarm ... In any case, there has never been a student who has been subjected to a viva due to concern regarding the source or indeed questioned. Some students have achieved first-class degrees through my writing for them ...

The article also includes statements about the responsibility resting with the student about how they use any material supplied and warnings about the stringent security arrangements for assessment procedures in universities.

Plagiarism by academics

The New York Times, 23 February 2002, describes how historian Doris Kearns admitted she 'borrowed some passages in her [1987] book' from several other books. The author claims her copying was 'accidental' and apparently arose when she 'confused verbatim notes with her own words'. The New York Times quotes her as saying, 'The mechanical process of checking things was not as sophisticated as it should have been.' The aggrieved author from whom Kearns lifted up to 50 phrases noted that 'adding quotation marks would have been a very messy editorial business, because there were so many of them.' The publishers have now destroyed all copies of Kearns' book.

Students' motivation for cheating

Think about:

- why do your students plagiarise?

- do you believe their explanations?

- how frequent is it?

- how might you find out?

Why does plagiarism happen?

At one time, getting a top grade was not of compelling importance to many undergraduate students. The employment market and graduate careers were such that most students with lower-second degrees did not feel themselves to be seriously disadvantaged. Nowadays many students feel that anything less than an upper-second-class degree will irretrievably damage their career prospects. At the same time, many have less time to study because they are in effect 'working their way through college' or coping with heavy caring responsibilities.

(McDowell and Brown, 2001)

Some academics dispute the relevance of studies on student motivation saying, 'I don't care why they do it, I just tell them it's not allowed and there are penalties for those who don't obey the rules.' As the definition of plagiarism cited on page 9 acknowledges, plagiarism is plagiarism, whether or not it is intended. On the other hand, Bannister and Ashworth (1998) claim that unless we understand 'the place and possible meanings of cheating within the student lifeworld' (p. 233), then attempts to understand the statistics and tackle the issue will be misguided.

Cox et al (2001) asked staff and students why plagiarism occurs and found that two-thirds of the respondents cited students' poor time management as the most common cause, with staff citing this much more frequently than students. The authors add that 'needing more help [was] also a popular choice.' Cox found that it was only undergraduates who cited the work being 'too hard' as a reason for cheating. Those who took this view constituted only a third of all respondents. The same study found that postgraduates and staff were much more likely than undergraduates to attribute cheating to poor supervision, to work not being checked, and/or to a low risk of being caught (but the frequency remained low at about 30% of the total). In general, academics offer both students' poor personal organisation and their lack of understanding as equally likely to underpin cheating behaviour.

Considering student motivation-

Either on your own or with colleagues, you could ask individuals to rank the 10 reasons given opposite in order of frequency for your/their students, then to compare with colleagues and with the research by Cox cited above and with comments on this exercise on page 92.

Alternatively ask the group to allocate responsibility for the situation highlighted. Such a discussion helps everyone move beyond 'blame the student' towards considering more effective teaching methods.

Reasons students give (not in order of frequency)	What might lie behind the statement
I got desperate at the last moment	poor personal time management; juggling multiple demands
I could not keep up with the work	poor personal time management; bunched assessments; multiple deadlines; poor information provided about deadlines
The tutor doesn't care so why should I?	perceived disinterest in the course content, in the student or in the student's learning; no enthusiasm shown by teacher; tutor using outdated or unchanged materials
I have to succeed – everyone expects me to succeed and I expect it, too	parental pressure; cultural expectations; costs of the course; living expenses; not being in employment, etc.
I don't understand what I'm expected to do to avoid plagiarism	unclear definitions; unclear instructions on referencing; lack of experience in (UK) academic writing
I can't do this! I'll have to copy	assignments perceived as beyond the student's ability; unclear assignment specifications; procrastination
I want to see if I can get away with it / I'll probably get away with it	testing the system; challenging authority; relatively minor penalties (or, if the 'penalty' is resubmission, a benefit!)
I don't need to learn this, I just need to pass it	prerequisites and mandatory courses that provide no intrinsic motivation; students with exclusively extrinsic goals, e.g. an award, certification
But you said, 'work together'!	misunderstanding of the role of collaboration in learning; misunderstanding of the need to submit individualised work for assessment; lack of shared understanding of what constitutes 'collusion'
But paraphrasing would be disrespectful / dangerous / nonsense	assumptions about how one treats experts – for example, amongst some international students, a lack of confidence in paraphrasing skills, especially in a second language

The reasons given for plagiarism in the table above are based on material in *Plagiarism Detection and Prevention*, the final report on the JISC electronic plagiarism detection project (Chester, 2001).

I often hear students say 'I deserve a 2.1.' They seem to regard work as currency and they are trading their time for a guaranteed result.

A university teacher

19

Lack of rhetorical confidence can easily lead to patching, when in fact the student has good content understanding. Such cases might need augmented modes of assessment such as a brief interview. Even the shift from 'plagiaphrasing' (unacceptable) to 'conventional academic writing' is not always clear, even to academics.

Biggs, J. (1999, p. 130)

I know what plagiarism is. We have it in Korea too, and we take it very seriously. I do not cheat deliberately. But I get into trouble when I write because I know some subject knowledge better than other and I can write it better. So the lecturer thinks I am cheating when it is my knowledge and I write it better than other times.

Student in the Errey study (Errey, in press)

International students' motives

> ### Think about:
>
> - are international students a special case?
> - do they have different motivations from home students?
> - how might you explain the higher rates of plagiarism in international students that are commonly reported in UK higher education?

Several reasons students give for plagiarism seem to apply especially frequently to international students, especially the belief that citing verbatim signifies respect for authority. Many academics describe how international students come from cultures where knowledge is held communally, available to all. Many international students do come from systems where memorising and reproducing information is highly valued (as, indeed, do many A-level students). Many come from countries where adherence to international conventions on copyright may be inactive or under-stressed. [Note: All countries with the exception of North Korea and Mayanmar have agreements to comply with the Berne conventions on copyright that underpin whatever local variations exist in particular states and territories.] Many also studied previously in settings where the norms and rules were different. For example, Walker (1998) reviews a study of postgraduates who 'made little attempt to conceal their [collusion] and argued that since their own cultural norms not only tolerated such behaviour but actually required it in the tradition of assisting a friend in need, it should likewise be tolerated by the … school' (p.93). But how well founded are British academics' explanations for the higher incidence of plagiarism in this group?

Research does not generally support the view that cultural differences make plagiarism more likely in international student groups. Errey (in press) interviewed 46 students from a wide range of countries in their third term of study in a UK university (undergraduate and postgraduate) and 30 academic staff who taught them. Each group offered very different explanations for plagiarism. Most of the academics cited cultural difference as the most common reason for students not complying with British conventions but none of the students did so. All the students knew that British universities would punish them if they plagiarised and most said they had similar rules in their home countries.

However, all the students in Errey's study, even after three terms of study, were unsure *how to act on this requirement* when writing coursework. (See Chapter 5 for more on teaching the skills and on the special needs of international students.)

So the high incidence among international students could arise from students cutting and pasting or downloading text, as this seems the best approach given their overwhelming need to succeed coupled with problems with meeting deadlines often arising from the work taking much longer than would be the case for UK students. Many non-native speakers of English avoid rewriting sources 'in their own words' even when they know this is expected, using a verbatim quote instead, from fear of losing the meaning through unskilful paraphrasing. Others say they do it because they find it hard to believe that the university wishes someone with imperfect English to rewrite the flowing prose of a native speaker (Angelil-Carter, 2000). Finally, it may be easy to explain why so many plagiarism cases involve international students: they are easier to catch. The most common sign academics use to spot plagiarism is change of writing style (much easier to do if the student is using a language other than their own).

Deliberate fraud

This kind of student sets out at the beginning of a course to cheat. He or she may employ a ghost writer or download an essay wholesale from the Web months before the coursework is due. Many academics view this kind of person as very rare or even imaginary, claiming it is much more likely that last minute panic triggers fraudulent action. Yet this supposed rarity attracts considerable concern – why? Perhaps there is undue interest from journalists who seek out these stories. Certainly when I am approached, journalists seem only interested in this aspect above all others. Perhaps teachers worry (correctly, I believe) that deliberate fraud would be hard to spot. It may also be that a small number of students who want to see if they can get away with plagiarism (or who broadcast their confidence in doing so) can have a poisonous effect, shaking other students' belief that the system is fair, reliable and worth their effort. However, as the use of the web grows, so too will the opportunities for wholesale downloading and systematic evasion of academic rules and conventions. Whenever I ask academic groups for their experience with fraudulent plagiarism, their response is a worried and near universal agreement that this is a small problem in some cases, a larger problem in quite a few, and a growing concern for everyone. We now need more systematic data gathering to confirm this perceived trend.

When I get nervous about writing up my thoughts in poor English even when I know the subject OK, I can't think. So I use other people's words.

Student in the Errey study (Errey, in press)

An overseas student said to me recently ' ... I copied the material straight from the Web because my English is not very good, and I wanted to make sure you understood what I was trying to say.'

Lecturer in HE

I was on the inter-site bus recently and overheard two students exchanging information on who to use locally to write coursework. They had detailed and up-to-date information on the going rates (£10 an hour, apparently) and who was best for what kind of work. I didn't intervene – they weren't in my school – but I did go back and suggest to my course team that we convene a meeting to talk about it.

A UK academic

Deliberate fraud

'I will definitely get someone else to do my project,' says Jo, a European student studying psychology in London. 'I don't know if I can afford it, but I'll try. I want a good degree.' Jo says she always relied on others to do her coursework. 'I usually get some help, but I know several people who pay their old teachers to write essays for them. A friend of mine paid £200 for a 2000 word essay. I think it's very common … to pay. All the people I know paid to get through the IELTS' (an English exam all foreign students must pass to qualify for British university study).

Extract from an online article by Stine Okkelmo that claimed 'one or two [such] cases every year' in the department cited.
http://www.hero.ac.uk/studying/archive/other_people_s_essays908.cfm
3 January 2002

Reasons to be cheerful

I usually find that colleagues are genuinely interested in the topic of plagiarism and enjoy thinking about it. Take, for example, the subheading of this section. Do I cite it because Ian Drury made it the title of a song? Probably not – but what if I used some of his lyrics? Then probably yes. Academic A asks, "Is it plagiarism to use coursework submitted for one course as the basis for coursework in another?" and Academic B responds, "It all depends what you mean by '…as a basis'". Nuances of meaning, disputed definitions, discipline-based understanding and unexplored assumptions often fascinate academics as much as they worry students. By seeking clarity and explicitness for themselves then by sharing this new understanding with students, academics can help students become true junior members of the academic community rather than assuming they already are. That's why this handbook offers materials for individual reading and for shared conversations and activities.

Tackling plagiarism can mean adopting a range of relatively straightforward approaches, using methods that a growing amount of experience shows can be effective. Best of all, changes designed to lessen plagiarism will probably increase the amount of effort and learning you can encourage from your students. Potentially, this is a win-win situation for you and for your students and therefore a legitimate reason to be cheerful.

Designing courses for deterring plagiarism

2

Some teachers advocate detection as the primary means for deterring plagiarism and research does suggest that students, too, see fear of being caught as 'one of the greatest deterrents' (Freewood, 2001). However, most teachers, even the most assiduous in checking for cheating, also see the benefit in changing their programmes and courses to make plagiarism less likely. This chapter suggests what you might design **in** to increase your students' chances of avoiding plagiarism, and how you might design **out** opportunities for easy plagiarism. But first, a word of warning: making any change on its own is unlikely to solve the problem of plagiarism. Only by adopting several suggestions, letting each strengthen and underpin the others and creating a sort of net of deterrence, will you make it more likely that students are learning, being assessed on their learning and avoiding shortcuts that bypass learning. Chapter 3 deals with specific aspects of assessment that could lessen plagiarism. Chapter 5 considers the teaching of skills that enable students to comply with academic conventions and do what a course asks of them.

Think about:

- what do you already know needs changing in the courses you lead?

- if you are redesigning a course soon, who do you need to work with?

- if you have collaborators, are they aware of the need to consider plagiarism?

Redesigning existing courses

Research on plagiarism supports the view that students are increasingly able to cheat, increasingly likely to submit work that is not their own, and increasingly unable to comply with academic rules and conventions (see Chapter 1). If your course was designed at a time when all these factors were easy to ignore, it would probably benefit from an audit now, so that specific ways to dissuade or deter plagiarism can be found.

An exercise in designing in and designing out opportunities for plagiarism

Building Bridges in Hot Countries

Learning outcomes for the course

As a result of this course, students will be able to:

- describe how to build long and short bridges;
- list factors affecting bridge construction in hot climates; and
- solve problems in building construction in hot countries.

Assessment:

- A 2,000 word essay on the last day of the course on either one of the following topics or one chosen by the student (40% of the final mark):

  1. Bridges in Ecuador;
  2. A history of bridge building in Nigeria; or
  3. How to build a bridge when the river floods a lot.

- A group project (45% of the final mark): the project will require a group of up to six students to produce a model of a bridge that would be capable of spanning a 50-ft chasm. The model must be able to fit on a phone book and must be made with the materials provided, i.e. matchsticks, string and card. Each group will be issued with the same materials. All members of the group will receive the same mark. All marks are awarded to the final product.

- Four case study reports of 500 words each (15% of the final mark): students will write up the weekly tutorial discussion of case studies after the session, submitting them the next week.

Some information about the course:

The course has run for the last five years in this format. Student projects are handed back at the end of term. Essays are not returned after marking. Case study material took considerable energy to develop because it uses examples that the lecturer experienced; they have not changed during the life of the course.

Plagiarism opportunity

a student could plagiarise any one of the assessments and not be any worse off for the rest.

Solution 1: integrate the tasks, perhaps substituting a computer simulation for the model and asking for a technical report that evaluates how successfully the simulated bridge was built; find a way to ensure that doing one task is necessary for doing the next.

Solution 2: test knowledge and skills – case studies could teach students to analyse situations and learn how to justify choosing certain actions; you could then test this learning in an unseen case study under exam conditions.

Collusion opportunity

all work is done out of sight.

Solution 1:
observe some work, perhaps instead of some of the lectures.

Solution 2:
require recording of activity and check it at specified times – logs, video diaries, threaded electronic discussions or project notes have been used (note: 'checking' does not mean assessing); peer checking might be possible and offers benefits (see page 33).

Plagiarism opportunity

the information requested is probably available on the Web or in a textbook in fully useable form.

Solution 1: work with this, asking students to demonstrate learning outcomes that value and require information gathering.

Solution 2: set tasks that ask students to find, compare and evaluate sites rather than simply plundering them.

Plagiarism opportunity

students could find one first, then 'choose' or choose a topic that suits a ghost writer's skills and knowledge.

Solution: don't allow last-minute changes.

Collusion opportunity

the whole group gets the same mark, regardless of individual contribution.

Solution 1: use the group task for learning but ask each person to submit something individually for assessment.

Solution 2: allocate some of the marks for peer assessment.

Solution 3: assess the process of building the model as well as the product itself.

Plagiarism opportunity

students could submit essays, case studies and models from previous years.

Solution: set new assessment tasks each time.

Plagiarism opportunity:

students could find essays or information on the Web.

Solution 1: essays are easily available – ask instead for technical reports or case studies from your own situation or data.

Solution 2: use evaluative or analytical essay topics.

Solution 3: set specific, recent or narrow topics; specify requirements such as which sources to include.

Plagiarism opportunity

essays are only seen at submission allowing last-minute downloading, copying or purchase.

Solution: ask for a plan, drafts or outlines – do not to mark them but sign and date them to verify they exist.

Plagiarism opportunity

anyone could have done the work that a student submits for assessment.

Solution 1: use vivas, in-class tests or oral presentations.

Solution 2: use observed meta-essays (see page 38).

New courses also need this kind of inspection. In either case, you might be too closely involved with the course to be able to detect opportunities for plagiarism. You may also be put off by worries about the time involved, and those new to course design may not be sure where to start.

One way to overcome reluctance to start reviewing your course is by considering a hypothetical example such as the one on page 24. You could also use this activity as a warm-up exercise if you share the redesign with a team of people. This course is called 'Building Bridges in Hot Countries'. Opportunities for plagiarism and collusion have been identified and possible solutions suggested.

Examples of designing out opportunities for plagiarism

Students are far less able to gain credit for work that is not their own (i.e. to plagiarise) in courses where there are:

- no chances to pass the course by submitting something that already exists;

- no chances to use others' work as evidence for assessment; and

- no processes for choosing and agreeing assessment tasks that might make fraud easy.

Examples of designing in aspects that will lessen plagiarism

Students plagiarise less on courses that include:

- links between assessment tasks so each builds on and confirms the rest;

- methods to track, observe and record student effort;

- acknowledgement of online information and encouragement to use online resources;

- ways for students to show individual effort and to create individual assessment artefacts;

- authentication exercises to ensure the student who gained the credit did the work; and

- opportunities for students to practise using academic writing skills, receive feedback and improve their practice.

I remember going into a lecture last year to observe and the handout still referred to xxx Polytechnic. I was embarrassed and the students just sniggered.

A lecturer in 2002

Suggestions for course design

Change the course requirements

This is perhaps the most straightforward place to start when considering how to lessen opportunities for plagiarism. Where essays have stayed the same year after year, the same case studies are issued (or only changed cosmetically by altering names or numbers), or when students are asked for tried-and-tested practicals, they are more likely to plagiarise. Franklyn-Stokes and Newstead (1995) confirm that students regard copying in such courses as simply common sense. Why should they make an effort when the lecturer does not?

Consider the learning outcomes

> ## Think about:
>
> - which are you asking students to do: to show they know or to use what they know?

Learning outcomes describe what students do to demonstrate their learning and the context within which their learning will be shown. Over the years, academics have developed a hierarchy of cognitive learning outcomes based on their complexity and derived from Bloom's taxonomy, named after its creator. Bloom's taxonomy describes how students learn by referring to different kinds of cognition. Each new level depends upon and therefore includes the previous ones, so assessing the higher levels (4, 5 and 6 below) will also check knowledge and comprehension.

Bloom's cognitive taxonomy:

1. Knowledge

2. Comprehension

3. Application

4. Analysis

5. Synthesis

6. Evaluation

Bloom's taxonomy is important when redrafting courses to lessen plagiarism because the lower levels (1 and 2: knowledge and comprehension), are much more likely to already exist. Asking students to 'show they know' can easily be interpreted as 'show you can find'.

Problem-based learning will not always produce active, investigating students. One study of medical students found that they didn't start by investigating their learning needs; they commonly started by "obtaining last year's objectives". The study also showed that students did not see this "undermining of the PBL ethics" as serious cheating.

Cogdell et al (in press) http://www.brookes.ac.uk /services/ocsd/1_ocsld/ isl2002/symopia/ Ashworth_symposium. html

Asking a student to explain, list or collect information is seen by some as an invitation to recycle someone else's solution. On the other hand, asking students to demonstrate learning outcomes that provide evidence of more complex thinking greatly lessens the chances that they will copy or purchase a document that already exists. Students will need to make an effort to show they can use information in a specified context or even evaluate someone else's use of it, perhaps provided in a case study. The more analytical, specific and creative the task, the less likely the solution already exists and therefore, for the student, the task becomes 'create the solution' not 'find the solution'.

As well as changing learning outcomes, you could add one for information gathering *per se*, including text and digital resources. Macdonald (2000) argues that collecting and using information is much closer to the employment experience of graduates than many others stressed in HE so it may also offer vocational value as well as encourage individual learning.

Create individualised tasks that result in individualised answers

Some courses set the same task for all students. Sometimes, this seems unavoidable because the skill is relatively straightforward, such as using an IT package or solving a practical problem. However, assessing application or comparison rather than use will encourage more individualised products. For example, instead of asking a question about patient care in general which might simply require all students to repeat back your lecture notes, ask students to identify a particular patient and consider how the general theory is relevant to that case.

The student's own experience

A Canadian lecturer, considering how best to deter plagiarism suggested setting assignments that 'use a personally relevant reference point such as the student's own home in architecture, own teeth in dentistry, family business in marketing, or favourite play in the theatre.' Instead of a theory, he suggests setting tasks arising from 'a model, proof, procedure, test or experiment.' For example, he asks students of psychology to 'select one of the ten personality theories listed in the course outline [and] apply it to your own personality. Evaluate the theory using yourself as the subject. What are its strengths and weaknesses with specific reference to your own personality? What, if any, is the applied value of this specific personality theory?'

Quoted in *Focus*, the in-house journal for Dalhousie University

When problems produce only one answer, they could be individualised after they have been completed by asking students to compare their solution with one you provide, perhaps explaining which one is more effective. By providing a range of incomplete or erroneous answers, you increase the variation of responses.

Finally, the whole task might be individually negotiated. McDowell and Brown (2001) advocate finding ways so:

> ... students are working towards divergent rather than convergent goals, by use of, for example, individualised negotiated assessments. Where students are meeting tutors over a period of time to discuss evidence of their achievement of required learning outcomes along individual pathways, it is difficult for them to produce anything which is not their own work.

They suggest that learning contracts can be used as a way of asking students to track what they learn and to establish an agreement between tutor and student.

Integrate assessment tasks

Think about:

- if students plagiarised some of the assessment, would that missing learning impact on their ability to do the rest of the course?

- if not, would that matter?

When able students were asked why they did not copy others' essays or download material, some referred to fear of detection. Others were confident they could do a better job than the 'stolen' essay. However, most said they didn't take shortcuts because coursework was necessary to their understanding. They knew they would need to demonstrate this understanding in another context, perhaps an oral presentation or in an exam. So whilst they looked at others' essays and admitted they often reproduced the structure, they wove in their own facts and arguments in order to 'get your head around it'. (Carroll, personal communication, 2001).

When asked why his department had no cases of plagiarism in the past year, a lecturer in a technical subject responded:

"Maybe it's because we know all the students but it's more likely because tasks don't lend themselves to cut-and-paste off the Web and copying is obvious. Students understand that coursework prepares them for exams and in statistics, we individualise work (i.e. same problem, different data)."

When coursework and exams crosscheck and reinforce each other, make this explicit - otherwise only the more strategic and successful students will spot the connection. Linking exams and coursework explicitly also raises the overall status of coursework. Research shows (Bannister and Ashworth (1998, p. 238) that students regard exams as:

> ... powerfully symbolic, with those occurring at the end of a period of study necessarily carrying a sense of dramatic climax. The perceived formality of the examination as an Occasion (sic) lends it gravity, as does its atypical and staged nature.

Assessment is covered in some detail in Chapter 3 because it is fundamental in deterring and dealing with plagiarism.

Build in overt structure to track student progress

Think about:

- how do you feel when a student submits a large piece of work like a thesis or dissertation that you have never seen until that moment?

- what do you currently do to ensure this is the student's own work?

Structure encourages all students to be as organised and strategic as the good ones. Evans (2000) opines that 'readers tend not to cheat and cheaters tend not to read' so designing in requirements to read and record the reading is likely to help. Designing in staging posts and requiring students to submit work for formative assessment will encourage forward planning. Several studies show that cheating and plagiarism are more common amongst weaker students with poor time-management strategies (Roig and deTommaso, 1995 and Bannister and Ashworth, 1998). Asking in stages to see and initial a plan, a draft and a final product can be helpful because last-minute panic may make plagiarism seem the only solution. One UK essay bank capitalises on this connection, offering free essays (with a disclaimer that users should 'never cheat or plagiarise in any way') under the heading Essay Crisis? What essay crisis! (http://www.revise.it). (Worried academics, faced with this idea, need to remember that checking that something exists is not the same as assessing it.)

'Richard' told journalists that essay banks are 'like a Napster for essays and coursework ... Usually it's just if someone has forgotten to do the work or has missed a deadline, then they will download and hand it in.'

Grossman, W. (2002) 'All their own work?', The Independent 15 April, 2002, p. 11

Using assessment to deter plagiarism

3

This chapter considers assessment issues and should be considered in conjunction with the issues raised under course design in Chapter 2. In general, suggestions focus on what you assess and how you manage the assessment process. It also discusses how you might structure tasks to ensure students understand what you want and to lessen opportunities for copying.

Giving students specific instructions

Harris (2001, p. 44) asserts:

> … clarity helps students understand what is expected of them and encourages them to do their own work because they feel more confident about exactly what to do … a major source of poor student papers (not just plagiarising) is the unclear assignment.

If you cannot tell yourself whether your instructions are clear, you could ask a colleague to comment; student feedback can also help when assessing and revising instructions. Even things which you take for granted might confuse students. Being explicit is especially important for some students such as international students who are not always used to decoding implied task instructions. I remember a colleague telling a story about a student in an exam interpreting the instruction to 'discuss' as an invitation to ask their neighbour, 'What do you think?'. The student did so – loudly.

Specific instructions also discourage students from reusing their own previous work (technically known as autoplagiarism or in some institutions, duplication).

As well as being specific about how students must approach the task, especially where collaborative learning might be involved, you could specify how students should designate shared work as distinct from individual contributions. For example, you might ask them to:

- write a preface describing who did what in a group report;

- cite each other in jointly written work just as they would library sources;

- use a device such as different colours to demarcate individual contributions in a shared artefact such as a poster; or

- conduct their discussions online using a threaded discussion package which dates and times individual contributions.

Using a signed statement of originality

In many institutions, students are routinely asked to sign (or better, compose and sign) a statement that asserts that the work is original, the result of individual effort, and written by the signatory. If the piece of work has arisen from collaboration, the contributions of each person could be acknowledged and described in an opening statement.

One example of a disclaimer

Students at Ruskin College in Oxford must submit a form with each piece of written work that includes an individualised statement that this particular work is their own, writing in the name of the paper, what it is for and who they are rather than simply signing a standard form. This is a fairly common requirement. What makes this form special is that it also includes a one-and-one-half page 'tutorial' on correct paraphrasing and use of quotes. The form includes a sample text, an unacceptable rewriting of the original and three different ways in which the original could be used acceptably (see also pages 54–55). The student thus has an opportunity, again and again during their programme, to learn these skills.

A statement might draw attention to specific rules and aspects that the marker views as essential as in this suggested wording (Harris, 2001 p. 60):

> I hereby affirm that (1) the research and writing of this paper are entirely my own; (2) I have not intentionally plagiarised any portion of this paper but have used quotation marks and citations appropriately; and (3) I have not helped any other student inappropriately by lending my notes, papers, disk, files or other materials.

Of course, many students sign such statements without thinking, just as most of us click the box saying we have read the agreements governing transactions before carrying out procedures online. However, asking for a signed statement might be one more link in the range of interventions which as a whole, could have an impact.

> **Think about:**
>
> - if you decided to start using a statement, who would need to be involved in the decision?
>
> - how would you inform the students about the purpose of the statements?

Asking for drafts

Academics say they are uneasy when a piece of work, especially one that carries a lot of academic weight like a dissertation or major project, arrives fully formed on their desk. How can they be sure the student him or herself was the author? Some pieces of work are large enough to warrant asking for drafts and if so, this either deters wholesale copying or lessens last-minute panic, a major cause of plagiarism. Soliciting drafts also helps students learn that good writers edit and revise their work using feedback from other students or from teachers. A more minimalist approach is to ask for drafts to be submitted alongside the final piece of work. Their existence is a reassuring sign of student effort.

Drafts for learning and deterrence

A course in geography originally required two essays, one towards the beginning of the course and one near the end. The tutor became increasingly despondent that despite all the time and effort spent marking and writing comments on the first essay, invariably there was little improvement in the second. The course now requires only one [essay]. First, students write a draft by a given date. In a seminar session, they are paired up and give detailed feedback to their partner who then redrafts the essay. When the essay is finally submitted it is accompanied by an account of how the feedback has been used, e.g. 'I've included more sources because the first draft was criticised for using only two. I've kept the introduction the same even though it was criticised as unclear because I don't agree...'.

As a result of this change the tutor has halved his marking load. It is true that only one topic is now assessed rather than two as before but the tutor believes that educationally this is more than compensated for by the following benefits:

- it develops the students' critical faculties;

- significantly better work is produced; and

- it is more like the 'real world' – good writing involves redrafting in the light of criticism.

[and it would deter plagiarism].

Rust (2001), LTSN Generic Centre publication

Asking students to assess each other using the teacher's criteria has many benefits including increasing the number of people keeping an eye out for plagiarism as in the example below:

Peer review to improve learning and spot plagiarism

A computing studies lecturer, faced with classes that doubled and doubled again in size, stopped marking essays himself. Instead, he instructed students to submit their work electronically, removed their names, assigned each student three essays to mark and provided the marking criteria. Students were then marked on the quality of the feedback they provided and how well they used the marking criteria. Several unexpected benefits ensued. The students were pleased their work was 'marked properly'(!), they wrote better essays themselves the next time, and they identified plagiarism in the unnamed scripts. Anonymity was crucial to calling attention to cheating.

Davies (in press)

Assessing the process as well as the final product

Even in a standard task, how the student arrives at an answer might vary even if the final result is largely similar. Sometimes the process is as relevant as the final answer and can, therefore, provide a more individualised artefact for assessment. In group work (which is a valuable learning tool and not one to be abandoned lightly), one way to deter collusion is to use the group activity to provide the learning but not as a sole source of assessment because communal effort can easily be exploited by freeloaders. If you choose to use group projects leading to assessment, think about:

- **requiring an individual record of what the group did**. This could be captured in contemporaneous logs (monitored, dated and initialled to ensure they are not made up the night before submission). Asynchronous online discussions produce a dated record of individual input for later review. Even minutes of group meetings usually show members' contributions.

- **asking for individual retrospective reflections on the group's work**. Log entries of group activity, rather than assessment per se, could provide material for individual writing on topics such as each person's contribution to the project (perhaps written under supervision, which allows you to compare answers for consistency and includes examples). Individuals could assert and illustrate their own learning arising from the project or evaluate the group's product (whatever it might be). A retrospective analysis of the problem-solving strategies used by the group (with examples from the group's experience, perhaps drawn from the log) can often cover very similar outcomes to the project itself. You could then allocate marks to reflect the relative importance of any one of these writing tasks for the student's final grade.

Create engaging assessment tasks

Students are often demotivated by carrying out academic work which seems to be purely routine, such as lab reports which have been done by many students before them, using the same equipment, with identical 'findings'. In this situation they can feel that there is nothing for them to contribute and that they are simply going through the motions … In comparison, students do value and take seriously assessment which appears to have some meaning … for example where they can see that they are developing skills and knowledge which will be relevant outside the university, or where they can express some choice and individuality in their work.

McDowell and Brown (2001, p. 7)

Setting criteria for assessment that take collaboration into account

Chapter 4 describes how one lecturer, in an effort to encourage collaboration and discourage collusion, stated clearly what was and was not acceptable. Here, the suggestion is to reward individuality and unique solutions by specifically mentioning them in assessment criteria. It is also helpful to state clearly whether assessment will take into account both the content and the language in which it is expressed. If not, is it acceptable for students to ask others to edit their work for grammar and vocabulary? You will help all students if you spell this out and you will especially address concerns of international students.

Reconsidering essay titles

Essays can be an effective and reliable way of assessing learning outcomes and the ability to write essays is seen as a valuable skill in its own right, particularly in some disciplines. However, because of their ubiquity and their longstanding popularity, academic essays are also more prone to plagiarism than other forms of writing. The essay banks and so-called paper mills listed on page 91 contain tens of thousands of possible titles offered for sale or for free. Both wholesale downloading and cut-and-paste plagiarism are possible and according to some authors, provide a real threat to final awards (Harris, 2001).

If you use essays, general or standard topics such as an essay on George Eliot, Napoleon or genetically modified food could be individualised (for example, by asking students to compare how an Eliot character and a recent public figure of their choice dealt with a situation). Because essay sites date quickly, asking for a recent event to be considered will greatly lessen cut-and-paste opportunities (for example, discussion of the impact of recent legislation on GM foods). Another way to narrow topics is to ask students to write about what did not happen. McKenzie (1998) suggests:

> ...instead of asking why events turned out particular ways in our past ... we might ask students to hypothesise why various outcomes did not occur [or] pose questions that have never been answered such as how do we restore peace in Northern Ireland?

This kind of task will inevitably produce more variety and will probably mean it is easier to spot collusion.

Using defined requirements and narrow task specifications

Furedi (2000) suggests that teachers 'demand that students engage with the literature provided by the course convener' as a way of deterring plagiarism. Harris (2001) in a very comprehensive and useful online paper, 'Anti-plagiarism strategies for research papers', suggests being very specific about requirements as in '... the paper must make use of two Internet sources, two printed book sources, two printed journal sources, one personal interview and one personally conducted survey' (p. 4). (Note: this very demanding set could be modified, of course, for lesser pieces of work!) Harris (2001) also mentions instructions such as:

- use one or more sources written within the past year;
- use one or more named books/articles; and
- incorporate the information provided [by the lecturer] such as data or cases.

One teacher, fed up with students copying from each other in a course teaching computer-assisted design, asked them to also make the object and submit it along with the design. He claimed that in the three years since they made this change, no students had copied because seeing two identical objects was instantly recognisable in ways that two identical designs apparently were not.

You might alter the task by asking students to use a mix of primary and secondary sources of information. Boehm (1998) suggests asking students to use interviews, surveys, questionnaires, email correspondence with experts and/or actual experience like attending a workshop as well as the more standard secondary sources when constructing an essay or research paper.

One simple way to check that a student's writing arose from research and reading would be to ask students to submit photocopies of the four or five most useful sources used in creating the report or essay. This is no problem for the student who writes his or her own paper and a headache for those who copied it.

Insist the students engage with the literature

Gregory Hanlon (2002) from the Department of History selects two research articles on a related topic and asks students to encapsulate the authors' arguments, note the means they used for reaching conclusions and explain why he (Hanlon) put them together. He requires students to avoid 'moralising' and to make their case in five pages (c. 2500 words). Hanlon claims the exercise, 'obliges students to write, rewrite and rewrite' and alerts them to the use of sources in history whilst avoiding 'making moral pronouncements on past societies' rather than being analytical. Critical material in all disciplines makes this assignment adaptable in fields other than history.

Using other methods of recording learning for assessment

Instead of an essay, you might ask for:

- **an annotated list of sources** – the list could be accompanied by comments on, for example, the reliability of the source, how the information was used in the group project, or how it is relevant to the topic;

- **an outline** rather than a finished product or a list of the resources that **would** have been useful (had the document been written) – both can go a long way towards showing understanding and knowledge;

- **skills-based** assignments where students must produce evidence of their competence;

- assignments that revolve around **case studies or scenarios**; Gajadhar (1998) claims these offer fewer opportunities for plagiarism; or

- **reflective journals and critical incident accounts t**hat record the student's own experience and that can 'be triangulated by [evidence from] a practice tutor or workplace mentor' (McDowell and Brown, 2001 p. 6).

You might also ask students to construct and display posters. This form of assessment encourages students to summarise, structure and select information.

Use skills-based assessments

A lecturer on a teacher training course attributes the low rates of plagiarism to several things including:

"drumming away at the need to reference. But mostly, it's due to asking students to write most assignments linked to their practice which, because it is often observed by tutors and school mentors, can easily be cross checked."

Tracking the programme as a whole will ensure students do practise and perfect valued academic writing skills but most students demonstrate many times that they can write essays before graduation. Asking for different kinds of work can significantly lessen the chances of submitted work being bought, faked or copied. More importantly, many of the above assessment methods are linked with deep learning and higher motivation so this is probably a win-win situation where both you and the students benefit.

Using assessment to verify authenticity

To check that the student's work has actually been done by the student rather than bought, copied, downloaded or recycled, you might organise:

- **a random viva of a percentage of the students.** If students know about this in advance, it might help deter some from attempting plagiarism. Oral exams can quickly identify whether or not students are able to talk about ideas and concepts covered in their work. They can also show that students who may not readily generate quick responses in class can discuss ideas they have had time to think through and organise in written form. However, if a viva suggests that a student might not be as familiar with the work as you would expect – perhaps because he or she is unable to explain technical or unusual words ('Tell me more about what you meant by iterative re-evaluation of the technological input.') – you may be moving from checking learning to checking suspicions of cheating. Comments on pages 71–72 may become important at this point.

- **an open-book test**. Open-book exams will of necessity push students to use knowledge gained through other activities in the course rather than reproduce it from memory or from copying.

- **an in-class or supervised task**. Evans (2000) suggests a meta-essay, written under supervised conditions on an undisclosed topic (for example, *Why I structured the essay in this way, Which sources were particularly useful, How I would do it differently next time, What I learned from writing it*). As well as checking authorship, a meta-essay encourages reflection and analysis. Alternatively, you could organise some of the sessions as supervised work time or observed activity.

Meta-essays

Diane Christian Boehm (1988) in her article, 'About plagiarism, pixels, and platitudes', describes how she asks students to write about their work as well as hand it in. She says, 'This reflection piece has in fact become one of my favourite parts of a writing assignment, for it gives me insights into my students' thinking and, since it is not graded or evaluated, creates a wonderful opportunity for dialogue about their development as writers.'

Informing students

4

Informing students about institutional requirements and academic conventions is a necessary (but not sufficient) step in ensuring they can comply with them. Actively teaching the skills is also usually needed and the next chapter will consider how you might teach students how to comply with copyright, to paraphrase properly, to cite others' ideas, and to abide by institutional requirements. This chapter is about how you might alert them to the need for any of these skills.

Think about:

- where and when do your students currently find out about plagiarism?

- is there any evidence that the current situation is ineffective?

- if there's no evidence on the current system, how might you find out if it's working?

Providing students with information about plagiarism is not easy. The information often has to compete with the mix of trivial and significant information that characterise the start of many programmes, and sometimes it is hard for students to judge which information is important. Students receive literally piles of documents or pieces of information at the start of a three-year degree programme and somewhat less for many postgraduate courses. One university has to ask the local municipal bin men to remain on standby to clear up discarded documents as students leave Freshers' Fairs and induction events for the Underground station. Students, like most of us, only attend to information when they need to – if then – so much induction is ignored.

Despite the relative ineffectiveness of providing information about plagiarism at induction, when sanctions are applied, many institutions tell students 'It's in the handbook' and report the comment is usually met with protests that the alleged plagiariser didn't understand the rules. It is probable that recent human rights legislation makes this situation contrary to natural justice and fairness, i.e. legally unacceptable. Even if this is not the case, it is no longer tenable under UK Quality Assurance Agency (QAA) codes of practice. In 2000, the QAA required institutions (amongst other things) to provide guidance on academic misconduct that is explicit and readily available.

Honing induction information

Induction sessions on plagiarism are usually brief – you may have only 15 minutes in a 'talking heads' type day or a portion of the first session in the programme to get the message across. Written information (either paper or Web-based) has the benefit of being accessible at any time but may make it even harder to capture students' attention. Whichever medium is used, you need to ensure the crucial facts are stated. Here are some suggestions:

- Link academic conventions to the values that underpin them. This helps to give students positive statements about what they are expected to do, not just negative ones of what they must not do. You might talk about a shared community of ideas and about respecting others' words and/or work in the same way as one might respect their more tangible possessions. Without understanding the basis for academic conventions, students see them as a form of good manners, like eating with the correct fork, or even as traps designed to catch them out. Although they may never embrace these values (and the studies on student motivation referred to in Chapter 1 show this is often the case), students can at least be introduced to the assumptions that form the basis of academic culture.

- Stress the link between good marks and attributing ideas and referencing before mentioning punishments. In universities, being able to find and use others' ideas to support your own argument is highly valued and their marks will reflect this in ways that were perhaps less explicit in students' previous education. A-level students, for example, are often trained for an exam where the rewards come for remembering and writing down a viewpoint, idea or fact but not necessarily for saying where it came from.

- Define and describe plagiarism and collusion without alluding to possible difficulties with the definition. A definition like:

    passing off someone else's work as your own, whether intentionally or unintentionally, for your own benefit

  may seem self-explanatory but studies show this is not the case. Freewood (2001) interviewed students in some depth on their understanding of plagiarism and found that:

while students appear to understand what plagiarism is and believe, in many cases quite strongly, that it is morally wrong, once you probe that understanding there can be confusion about what really constitutes plagiarism and what the university and individual tutors will find acceptable. Only providing information on referencing systems does not tackle this confusion.

- Tell students where they can go for more help and information – this may be the most important message of all. They are unlikely to attend to information about academic conventions until they need to, perhaps when they produce a piece of work. Where can they check assumptions:

  - in the handbook?
  - with a personal tutor?
  - on a Web site, either the institution's or one of those suggested on page 91?
  - in specialised handouts, perhaps from a student services department or the library?

  Ensure you also mention learning support staff, teachers of English for academic purposes, or peer tutoring arrangements with more experienced students if these are provided by your institution.

Use activities to underline your message

I followed up a presentation that was given to 100 first-year students at induction and found that, six months later, they remembered the session for how they felt about hearing the information, but not what was said (Carroll and Pepperell, 2002). This does not mean the presentation was wasted effort – students may need many reminders and all opportunities should be used. However, even a brief exercise that asks them to use the definition would reinforce the message at induction.

1. Present cases like the following and ask which describe plagiarism:

   Case 1 – a student asks a friend to see her essay, notes down the structure and jots down the main idea in most of the paragraphs. She then goes home and writes her own essay based on the lecture notes.

   Case 2 – a student writes an essay full of quotes from other authors with each one credited.

   Case 3 – student downloads four paragraphs from the Web, writes down the Web site after the section and includes the four paragraphs verbatim in a three-page paper. No quotation marks.

2. Ask students to do the 'draw the line' exercise below:

Where do you draw the line?

In the examples below, number 1 is plagiarism and number 6 is not. Where do you draw the line?

1. Copying a paragraph verbatim from a source without any acknowledgement.

2. Copying a paragraph and making small changes – e.g. replacing a few verbs, replacing an adjective with a synonym and including the source in the list of references.

3. Cutting and pasting a paragraph by using sentences of the original but omitting one or two and putting one or two in a different order, no quotation marks; in-text acknowledgement e.g (Jones, 1999) plus inclusion in the reference list.

4. Composing a paragraph by taking short phrases of 10 to 15 words from a number of sources and putting them together, adding words of our own to make a coherent whole; all sources included in the reference list.

5. Paraphrasing a paragraph with substantial changes in language and organisation; the new version will also have changes in the amount of detail used and the examples cited; in-text acknowledgement e.g. (Jones, 1999) and inclusion in the reference list.

6. Quoting a paragraph by placing it in block format with the source cited in text and list of references.

Based on an exercise in *Academic Writing for Graduate Students* by John M. Swales and Christine B. Feak, University of Michigan (1994).

See page 92 for comments on this exercise.

3. Ask new students to create scenarios, either in small groups or as a whole to illustrate the definition, based on imagination or instances they have encountered; for example, given the word 'duplication', they might produce: 'Andy wrote a paper for a first-year course that got a good grade and submitted the same paper in year three where it got a C.'

4. Do a brief version of the exercise like that described on page 52 asking students to link words/phrases like incorrect referencing, plagiarising, creating data or colluding to descriptions of students' actions;

5. Ask students to create answers for some FAQs like these (see pages 49 and 51 for the origins of these quotes):

- Why can't I use the textbook author's words if they are better than any I could think of?

- What difference does it make if I just put it in the bibliography?

- It is my work. I've changed the words in the article to my own. Isn't that enough?

- There are that many opinions out there that somebody has already thought of whatever I might write. If I say something that is original and somebody else somewhere has already come up with it, will I be done for it?

Think about

- do you specifically mention collusion with students?

- is there any evidence they find this concept confusing?

- are you clear in your own mind what constituites collusion?

Defining collusion and informing students

Whereas many staff and students find defining plagiarism difficult (see Chapter 1), almost everyone has difficulty identifying where collaboration stops and collusion begins. More often than not, students are given instructions such as, 'Work in a group but each of you must submit your own work.' It is relatively common to see peer instruction valued in class only to have students meet with dire consequences when they use it in assignments. Most find this confusing and need clear guidelines and clear definitions. Comments on collusion throughout this handbook might help you construct guidelines for your own students or you might build on an example like the one on page 44, created for a masters-level course with a very high percentage of non-native speakers of English.

Case study on informing students about collusion:

'I always include hands-on stuff on collusion but don't call it that. Usually, I call it 'Acceptable English language editing and correction for written assessments'. I provide a handout specifying what is acceptable and what is not acceptable (see below). We then examine specific cases and I finish by showing the students how they can cite each other in their work just as they would cite books in the library.'

A UK lecturer on a postgraduate course

Handout:

It is acceptable to:

- ask for help from other students or people outside the course in improving your written English language;

- ask friends or other students for comments on work you do not submit for a mark;

- ask others for feedback in practice writing sessions;

- ask for general comments on your strengths and weaknesses in written English;

- approach the English Language Centre on campus, to use their services, and attend their training; and

- self-assess your own work through looking at that of others.

In this course is not acceptable to:

- ask someone outside the course to read and correct written work you intend to submit as your own, even if the corrections are only confined to the English language components of the work – both content of the work and the way in which you write about the ideas must be your own work; or

- submit work for assessment that is not your own – submitting work that is done jointly by you and by others is collusion.

Continuing to offer information

Information about what constitutes plagiarism and how to conform to good academic practice needs to be offered throughout a student's academic career using course handbooks, dissertation cover sheets, assignment briefing sheets, and user-friendly leaflets. Some postgraduates as well as the more strategic undergraduates find that institutional instructions on referencing and definitions of plagiarism are effective (although students from both these groups have told me they would have welcomed more specific instruction on citing Web sites, noting these sites frequently change or die). Where no guidance existed, these students said they reverted to whatever rules applied in their discipline-based journals. They recognised the importance of using correct citations outside the university as there are few spotters of published plagiarism more vigilant than the original author.

Diagnosing the level of student need

Where academic writing skills are particularly important, you may want to invest time and effort at the induction stage into checking students' skills and ensuring they have a realistic sense of their own abilities. An online self-testing or self-teaching package, either created by the institution or using a commercial package such as the Glatt plagiarism teaching package (http://www.plagiarism.com) could be useful. Many higher education institutions provide extensive Web-based programmes on plagiarism, such as:
http://www.library.ualberta.ca/guides/plagiarism.

Many include exercises or quizzes, such as:
http://education.indiana.edu/~frick/plagiarism

or you might put some of the exercises in this handbook online. One institution requires students to log on and complete the activities in the first three weeks of their course. Another makes it a requirement before students can receive a grade for the first piece of work in the first term.

Another approach is to solicit samples of students' work when they first arrive. Students often complain that they receive no feedback on whether or not their writing is acceptable until they are graded on it. Early practice, perhaps using peer assessment, is often welcome, offering the chance to use assessment criteria, marking each others' efforts or trying out exercises such as the suggestions on checking others' citations (see page 53). Of course, the teacher him or herself could see practice work and comment on it rather than asking students to check each other. This has two disadvantages: less learning for students and more work for teachers. A middle ground might be to sample the students' efforts and provide general feedback to the group

We had one lecturer in the first year who really spelled out what to do and what not to do about plagiarism in the course handbook. There were rules, examples, even a bad example. I kept that handbook beside me for the next three years when I was writing something. It was crucial.

Final year student

along the lines of 'many of you missed examples of paraphrasing that should have been cited.' A practice exercise might help students see that academic regulations apply to them in their writing, not just to a theoretical situation.

Encouraging fellow academics to become interested in plagiarism

I assume because you are reading this book that you are interested in plagiarism. However, you may need to encourage fellow academics or students to also take an interest in the issues and skills described in this handbook. Some of the activities described below would work best in a group; all are designed to spark interest or alert others to the need to pay attention to plagiarism:

- **give examples of quotes from students using cheat sites** – many have discussion boards attached that serve as chat rooms or collect quotes from this book;

- **use cartoons** or news clippings – a quick search on Google will produce recent online stories; or

- **organise a virtual tour of paper mills** using the urls on page 91. This could be unstructured individual exploration or something more organised like a 'treasure hunt' exercise ('find an essay on Emily Bronte as a feminist writer') with prizes for the first to produce a result.

> *I found that, again and again in disciplinary interviews, accused students acknowledged that their attention has been drawn to University regulations, and to the relevent scholarship. The problem is that when offences are committed, students are not relating regulations to their own behaviour, because they have no dishonest intent. They do not see citation conventions as essential devices ... but as niceties on a par with punctuation.*
>
> *An experienced academic charged with disciplining students accused of plagiarism*

Think about:

- if you used any of these suggestions, when might they be appropriate?

- who do you need to approach to discuss induction matters?

- who could work with you on this?

Teaching the skills

5

The previous chapter discussed how a short session on avoiding plagiarism might be handled. Such a session, often offered as a lecture to a large number of listening newcomers, has obvious limits in tackling plagiarism. A short talk may be effective at conveying information, but cannot change attitudes and beliefs or develop skills (Bligh, 1998). Wilhoit (1994), writing before the explosion of electronic sources, states that the majority of students fail to comply with regulations because they do not understand them. Many academics explain the prevalence of misuse of paraphrasing and referencing by claiming that students do not know how to reference. Many have been taught that it is perfectly acceptable to copy and thinly paraphrase work from secondary sources. You will need to get students actively involved and devote time to discussion if you wish to overcome the misconceptions and lack of awareness that most students bring to higher education.

Think about:

- how do your students currently learn about plagiarism?

- which students find this sufficient?

- which students need more help?

Induction or apprenticeship?

One way to cope with students' early confusion might be to apply a period of exemption, allowing first-year students (for example) to learn and practise referencing skills and labelling shortfalls as 'poor academic practice'. Certainly many institutions offer students an informal apprenticeship during which those who plagiarise warrant a comment in feedback ('this should be referenced or it will lose you marks'). Some students may even be offered the opportunity to correct the work and re-submit – this is, in effect, a reward as it offers them an extension. I have heard academics justify this state of affairs as necessary owing to students' weak writing skills, their rudimentary awareness of referencing and inexperience in reading for research purposes. Staff claim that asking too much too soon discourages students and lecturers alike, often stating, 'If we're too strict, everyone will fail.'

Other academics (and some institutions) take the view that using others' ideas as one's own for personal benefit constitutes plagiarism no matter when it happens or who is doing it. A senior manager in one university that operates a 'no grace period' told me that almost all students claim their plagiarism was unintended and resulted from misunderstanding of the rules, with PhD candidates being among the most vociferous in this regard. My own university takes the view that ignoring plagiarism, even for what looks like benevolent reasons, encourages students to put off learning about referencing and paraphrasing. We even worried that some would see losing a few marks as a price worth paying for an easier life in their first year. Delay also reinforces the view that academic rules are more about avoiding punishment or being polite than they are about upholding the values of academic discourse. If universities constitute a community of thinkers who build on and acknowledge each other's ideas and if students are junior members of that community, then letting students 'break the rules' whilst offering guidance for the future is inconsistent with academic values and therefore wrong. Plagiarism avoidance is as important as any other academic skill we wish students to develop.

Delaying action on plagiarism is probably ineffective as well as misleading. Studies show that many students don't collect coursework once they know the mark they have been given and do not read corrections and feedback on their work. Those who do receive feedback seem rarely to adapt their practice to comply with well-meaning advice or to correct previously held incorrect ideas. One study (Fritz et al, 2000) explains the ineffectiveness of this feedback by claiming that the effort and time that went into making the error was more memorable and significant to the student than the subsequent correction. Treating all plagiarism as unacceptable means students use the early years to learn the skills rather than delaying until it 'matters'.

It is important to remember that plagiarism can be identified without implying maximum penalties for offenders. The question 'is it plagiarism?' is separate from the question, 'what happens as a result?' See page 74 for suggestions about determining fair punishments, especially at the start of programmes.

Think about:

- are the skills students need to avoid plagiarism actually taught in your programme?

- if so, where does this happen?

Teaching academic conventions

It can be problematic to find time to teach students how to avoid plagiarism, especially in modularised programmes. Compulsory modules are likely to be 'full' of discipline-specific content, but confining teaching to optional modules would mean students either miss it or encounter it several times. To cope with this difficult problem, many programmes default to implicit strategies, expecting students to pick up the skills as they go along. Happily, the more strategic do so. It may also be that the growing emphasis on explicit learning outcomes and on informing students more clearly about all their responsibilities will help all students teach themselves these skills. However, those who read very little, who come from a background where different writing skills were rewarded (see Chapter 1) or those whose skills are poorly developed for whatever reason will need practice to master academic writing skills. 'Stressing the dire consequences of failing to observe official guidelines, in the absence of constructive and positive guidance, may have a "crippling" effect on the academic confidence of students' (Bannister and Ashworth, 1998 p. 239).

Below are some alternatives to the trial-and-error approach:

1. **making the skills a compulsory element of the programme** – for example, the English Department at Oxford Brookes is devising a compulsory first-year module on academic writing for their own students; it will include practice in citation and acceptable paraphrasing;

2. **offering a compulsory generic course on study skills**, often broadening the syllabus to include writing for academic purposes, library use etc. – for example, all students in one higher education institution in the Midlands must complete a half-module on study skills in their first year, offered at several different times in both semesters; the course content includes academic writing skills;

3. **incorporating skills into discipline-based teaching** – for example, the Publishing Department at Oxford Brookes University analysed the programme to check which modules taught students how to write an acceptable report; course regulations were changed to ensure students encountered at least one of these modules in the first year; and

4. **providing optional academic support and guidance sessions** – for example, DeMontfort University offers online resources and handouts covering key skills such as time management and advice on avoiding plagiarism; students are told of this resource at induction.

How misunderstanding blocks creativity

There are that many opinions out there that at some stage somebody might have thought of ... I have the feeling that if I said something original [the assessor] will say somebody else has said this before you so why haven't you acknowledged them? ... it's a bit worrying about trying to come up with something original.

A first-year student, quoted by Freewood (2001)

49

Each approach has difficulties. Numbers 1 and 3 risk triggering arguments about diluting content, about where these skills are best taught, and about who is best able to teach them. Generic 'study skills' courses, whilst often championed in programmes that take students from diverse backgrounds, are often seen by students as a distraction from their primary goal of a discipline-based qualification – those most likely to benefit are also most likely to see such courses as an additional burden. Generic 'study skills' teachers struggle with adapting what they offer to a wide range of disciplines and widely variable requirements depending on the contexts where students will use the skills. On balance, designing in compulsory teaching sessions on academic writing and citation skills where students can apply the skills to discipline-specific content as part of their core assessment tasks is the most likely way to ensure students learn and use academic citation conventions.

Many inexperienced students welcome the idea of attending additional instruction in writing for academic purposes in the form of classes, surgeries or drop-in clinics. Help is especially useful if it does not stigmatise the student and is offered at a range of times, as flexible scheduling reduces the chances of compromising students' other work. It is also helpful if the person offering support is a specialist attuned to the needs of particular groups such as mature students, dyslexic students or international students. Supplemental help will need forceful marketing as the students most in need are also those least adept at seeking it out. Resources allocated to this work should reflect the sensitive and often extended nature of this kind of support, especially for international students.

Activities for teaching academic writing skills

To avoid plagiarism, students need to be able to:

- differentiate what needs attribution from what does not;

- use in-text citation conventions;

- create appropriate reference lists and in some cases, bibliographies;

- attribute direct quotes using an acceptable convention such as quotation marks, indented paragraphs, a different font or italics;

- paraphrase and attribute others' words and ideas; and

- use footnotes.

We used to run workshops for students on writing skills but they didn't come. Now we employ a retired academic for four mornings a week to be in the reception area outside the school office. Most who ask for help are international students but anyone can. In the school, he's known as 'the man who sits' and we think this is a better use of scarce tutoring resources.

A UK undergraduate programme leader

Questions show student confusion

One department collected the most common questions they encounter from students regarding plagiarism. The responses demonstrate how difficult students find complying with academic conventions. FAQs included:

- Why can't I use somebody else's words if they are better than any I can think of?

- I put the source in the bibliography. Why do it in the text, too?

- What if I can't remember which book I got it from?

- Why use a 'reference'? I said which person had the idea originally.

- I said it was in the *Times*, 1999. Surely that's enough?

- We were taught at school to copy huge chunks out of books. Why is it wrong?

- Does it really matter if I just forget?

- It is my work because I have changed the words in the article to my own so I don't have to reference, do I?

- How closely does one piece of work have to resemble another to be plagiarism?

- How can I not get caught?

Carroll, personal communication, 2001

Students cannot learn how to do these things by listening to lectures which lay out the rules; they need to practise and receive feedback as to whether or not they did so acceptably. Freewood (2001) notes that students often express confidence in their understanding of plagiarism yet once you probe, there can be confusion. Students she interviewed confirmed the need to talk with an academic in a tutorial-type environment where students can ask questions. She also found evidence of the importance of a good relationship with academic staff in helping students raise concerns about plagiarism. In whatever setting you decide to teach these skills, the following activities could be used.

1. To ensure students know the difference between cheating in general and plagiarism and collusion in particular, you might offer a list of behaviours like the one below, based on research done in 1995 by Franklyn-Stokes and Newstead and updated with reference to the Web. All are cheating but only some are plagiarism.

Comments on this exercise are on page 92.

Differentiating cheating behaviours

Ask students to identify which actions would constitute plagiarism, defined as 'passing off someone else's work as your own' and which are examples of collusion, defined as plagiarism where the work is that of a fellow student.

1. Allowing your own coursework to be copied by another student.

2. Taking unauthorised material into an exam.

3. Fabricating references or a bibliography.

4. Lying about medical/other circumstances to get special consideration.

5. Copying another student's coursework with their knowledge.

6. Buying coursework from an essay bank or a 'ghost writer'.

7. Taking an exam for someone else or vice versa.

8. Illicitly gaining information about the contents of an exam.

9. Inventing data (for example, making up answers to a survey).

10. Not contributing a fair share to group work that is assessed for a group mark.

11. Ensuring the availability of books/journals in the library by deliberately mis-shelving them or cutting out chapters/articles.

12. Paraphrasing material from a source without acknowledging the original author.

13. Copying material for coursework ... without acknowledging the source.

14. Copying from a neighbour during an exam.

15. Altering data (for example, making the results of a survey seem more favourable).

16. Doing another student's coursework for them.

17. Submitting jointly written coursework as if it was an individual piece of work.

The list of behaviours above is based on Franklyn-Stokes, A and Newstead, SE (1995).

Note: You could also use this list to check student understanding of other words such as cheating, collusion, plagiarism, impersonation, duplication, and falsification of data by asking them to match the word to the appropriate behaviour.

2. To teach students when they must use a citation, issue students with an academic essay, either written specially for the exercise or obtained by exchanging essays within the cohort. Ask students singly or in small groups to review the work, checking whether or not the rules listed below have been followed.

Citation rules

The statements in bold are offered as rules students must follow. The questions in italics could be used to guide students in reviewing an academic essay.

These must be marked with a citation:

- **direct quotations**
  – does any of it read like it is someone else's words other than the student writer? Has the author indicated direct quotations correctly by using, for example, indented paragraphs, quotation marks or a change of font?

- **paraphrases and summaries of others' ideas**
  – if the writer could not be expected to have created this idea, is it cited?

- **arguable assertions, i.e. anything controversial or not clearly factual**
  – is anything not cited which a student could imagine themselves disagreeing with or debating?

- **statistics, charts, tables and graphs** from any source, even if the writer created the graph using material from another source.

These do need not to be marked with a citation:

- **common knowledge** – if a wide spectrum of readers are familiar with an idea or its truth is generally accepted, you need not cite it; quotations, paraphrases or summaries attributable to a specific source, however, should still be cited if at all possible – no matter how widely known.
  Is anything cited unnecessarily?

- **facts** available from a wide variety of sources – if a number of textbooks, encyclopedias or general reference sources include an idea you wish to use in your text, you need not cite it; you can still increase your credibility, however, by citing; most statistics should be cited.
  Are any facts not cited that might usefully be so?

- **your own ideas, discoveries or words** (excluding, of course, words based upon another's words or ideas).

Source: Based on information offered by Sherri Wahrer to American students on http://www.bgsu.edu/offices/acen/writerslab/handouts/plagiarism.htm (July 2002)

3. To teach students how to use correct citation conventions, offer examples of acceptable and unacceptable practice such as the following extract from Ruskin College mentioned in Chapter 4:

Unacceptable practice

The material in italics in the following paragraph has been taken from Eric Taplin, The Docker's Union, Leicester University Press, 19085, pp. 166–7. If students use these ideas without a statement of where they come from, as in the version below, this would be plagiarism.

> ... James Sexton of the National Union of Dock Labourers was a good example of a trade union leader who became a reformist. His *views were moulded by his industrial experience. He always claimed that he was an agitator and a socialist but he was increasingly at home among the reformist trade union establishment. With the foundation of the Labour Party his allegiance to the more radical ideology of the ILP waned. His socialism was never much more than a search for enlightened reforms to better the conditions and standard of living of working people. Such modest aims put him increasingly at odds with the more radical elements within the Liverpool labour movement.* The same story could be told about many other trade union leaders whose careers started in the late nineteenth or early twentieth centuries.

Examples of the proper use of this material would be:

Acceptable practice

> James Sexton, the Liverpool dockers' leader, was an example of a trade union leader for whom, 'socialism was never much more than a search for enlightened reforms to better the condition and standard of living of working people.' [1] As a result, when the Labour Party was formed he drifted away from the ILP and its more radical outlook. The same story could be told about many other trade union leaders whose careers started in the late nineteenth or early twentieth centuries.
>
> [1] Eric Taplin, The Dockers' Union, Leicester University Press 1985, p. 167.

or:

Acceptable practice

As Taplin (1985, pp. 166-7) has pointed out about James Sexton, the Liverpool dockers' leader's:

> views were moulded by his industrial experience. He always claimed that he was an agitator and a socialist but he was increasingly at home among the reformist trade union establishment. With the foundation of the Labour Party his allegiance to the more radical ideology of the ILP waned. His socialism was never much more than a search for enlightened reforms to better the conditions and standard of living of working people. Such modest aims put him increasingly at odds with the more radical elements within the Liverpool labour movement.

The same story could be told about many other trade union leaders whose careers started in the late nineteenth or early twentieth centuries.

or:

Acceptable practice

James Sexton, the Liverpool dockers' leader, was an example of a trade union leader for whom socialism never amounted to much more than an aspiration to improve the conditions of life for working people, through reforms. As a result, when the Labour Party was formed he drifted away from the ILP and its more radical outlook (Taplin, 1985, pp. 166-7). The same story could be told about many other trade union leaders whose careers started in the late nineteenth or early twentieth centuries.

Bob Purdie, Examinations Officer, Ruskin College, July 1996 (used with permission)

4. Once students are alerted to ways to cite others' ideas, check they can paraphrase by offering acceptable and unacceptable versions of the same text as in the example below, taken from a site maintained by the University of Alberta Libraries.

Acceptable and unacceptable paraphrasing

This exercise is designed to teach 'proper paraphrasing' using a text by Thomas Flanagan entitled *Riel and the Rebellion: 1885 Reconsidered* and using a convention which numbers citations and lists them at the end of the work. The verbatim text reads:

> *However, the true importance of the Rebellion in our history is more symbolic than military. It will always be remembered because it expressed several of the fundamental tensions of Canada: the aspirations of western settlers to run their own affairs versus the desire of Ottawa to control the public domain according to its own conceptions of the national interest; the conviction of natives, both Indians and Metis, that this was 'their land' versus the belief of Canadians in British sovereignty; the conflicting sympathies of English and French Canadians towards the French-speaking, Catholic Metis; the desire of some in the west for union with the United States; and the quite realistic fear among Canadian statesmen that American annexation would follow if Canada did not have a strong presence on the prairies.*

Two re-writes are offered:

(i) The importance of the Red River Rebellion is not due to its military aspect but the symbolic one. The rebellion will be remembered because it revealed several things about Canada. First, the rebellion revealed the tension between the need for Ottawa to control the west and the western settlers' need to control themselves, or join the United States. Second, the conflict showed the division between the Natives and the other Canadians who believed in British sovereignty, and the division between the English and French Canadians towards the French-speaking, Catholic Metis. Third, the rebellion revealed the fear of some politicians that the Americans would take over the west if Canada did not settle the prairies.

(ii) The Red River Rebellion will be remembered by what it revealed about the insecurities of a fledgling nation and the conflicts among her people. In the west, the settlers aspired to independence from a domineering government in Ottawa while some of the more radical settlers wished to join the United States. Further conflict existed between the Natives, who viewed the land as theirs, and the Canadians who perceived the land as an extension of British ownership and governance. Other sources of tension were found between the differing English and French perceptions of the plight of the French-speaking, Catholic Metis. Omnipresent during these conflicts was the fear that the United States could readily subsume the Prairies (Flanagan 4).

The student is then asked which is not plagiarism because:

1. proper acknowledgement for the ideas presented in the passage is given; and

2. the writer uses his or her own words.

And which is considered plagiarised because:

1. only the wording of a few phrases was changed and the sentences were only re-arranged; and

2. the writer does not acknowledge the source of the information and ideas.

http://www.library.ualberta.ca/guides/plagiarism/

Once students can differentiate between acceptable and unacceptable paraphrasing, ask them to paraphrase brief extracts themselves then check their efforts using peer review. You might suggest non-native speakers of English build in an intermediate step: explaining the text to a friend who writes it down. Moving from written text to speech often removes the strong pull towards using the original authors' phrases and words.

Pages 90–91 list many sites which offer similar activities and guidance

Helping students understand how academics assess their work

Students who have used and discussed criteria are far more likely to use them to guide and shape their own submissions. Price et al (2000) demonstrate that getting students to use criteria themselves rather than just reading them in a course handbook is a key element in ensuring students understand what is valuable in their work One way to encourage this is to use essay banks and 'cheat' sites (see page 91 for urls). This suggestion is viewed by some academics as provocative, possibly helping students cheat. Others regard it as naïve to believe students are unaware of such 'services', drawing an analogy with arguments against sex education. As well as helping students understand 'the academic game', asking them to mark essays available for sale will demonstrate their generally low quality and high cost (Olsen, 1998). I have looked in some detail at a large number of such sites and find the quality generally very poor indeed. (See also pages 34 and 35 for peer review exercises.)

Think about:

- how important do you see spending time on academic writing and avoiding plagiarism compared to all the other things students must master?

- which of your students will need more than you can offer?

- how can you encourage them to get the help they need?

Reinforcing understanding for particular groups

Some students need to set aside skills and assumptions that served them well in previous educational settings and learn complex new ones. For example, students might have been rewarded for reproducing large chunks of others' texts as a way of signalling they know of the existence of this information (Ryan, 2000). This is especially common in some A-level syllabuses and in international students' previous education. Angelil-Carter (2000, p. 165), discussing the needs of South African students, reminds her fellow academics that these students often:

> … are immersed in highly religious cultures … oral history and [a] literature tradition that requires and values accuracy of memorisation. The student who is plagiarising may simply be making use of the modes of textual construction that he or she knew at school.

Training students to operate as researchers

Teachers hope that training students in research methods will benefit the students themselves. The skills of inferring, deducting, deriving meaning from context, and forming hypotheses have value far beyond their application to scholarly research. If these skills are neglected, de-emphasised or misunderstood, something significant in the educational process will be lost. Technology [can be] misused to create shoddy imitations of responsible scholarship [rather than] a nuanced and judicious selection of sources to produce a coherent and persuasive whole … Instructors can model the process through lectures and guided discussions and can illustrate the difference between the critical use of sources and the arbitrary recitation of random references from a database … When the instructor promotes a climate of authentic ownership of texts and ideas, it will be easier to discuss the differences between genuine scholarship and the mere assemblage of cannibalised references that create the illusion of thoughtful research.

Mirow and Shore (1997, p. 43)

Many international students 'borrow' the words of native authors through lack of confidence in their own abilities to write correct, clear English. Watkins and Biggs (1996, p. 279), commenting on Chinese students, notes:

> Students who want to make a point particularly clearly see paraphrasing the source as a strange thing to do when the source itself makes the point better than they ever could reword it in an imperfectly mastered language.

Gathering ideas and quotes from a wide range of sources to construct an argument or evaluate the reliability of the information is valued in the UK but some international students find it both strange and disrespectful, especially if they come from academic cultures where offering personal and possibly critical views is not acceptable.

Setting aside previously successful strategies and learning new ones can take considerable time and effort but where task requirements are made very explicit, many students adapt quickly (Volet and Kee, 1993 and Errey, in press). Where requirements remain implicit and no help is provided, some struggle for years. Even with explicit information, many need specialist help (Fox, 1994). Many authors of books on teaching in HE address the teaching of international students explicitly, including reference to plagiarism (see, for example, Ryan, 2000).

Stages students use to develop their writing skills

Wilson describes four stages of writing that non-English speakers adopt:

- **Repetition**: simple copying from an unacknowledged source. [This happens when the student is] not confident of the content area. **Unacceptable.**

- **Patching**: copying, with joining phrases, from several sources. [This happens when a student offers] some general, non-specific acknowledgement. Still **unacceptable** but harder to spot.

- **Plagiphrasing**: paraphrasing several sources, and joining them; all sources are in the reference list, but pages unspecified. **Unacceptable**.

- **Conventional academic writing**: ideas taken from multiple sources and repackaged to make a more or less original and relational synthesis. Quotes properly referenced, general sources acknowledged. [This happens when the student is] quite confident of what is being said and able to create a new 'package' even if none of the ideas are new.

Biggs, J (1999) *Teaching for Quality Learning in Higher Education* p. 129 (OUP) quoting Wilson (1997)

Making the time

Sometimes, it is hard to remember how confusing, challenging and alarming students find these matters, especially if you have been using academic conventions and assumptions successfully for years. You need to plan in time for discussion, practice and feedback as well as for information giving. Active learning methods add to students' knowledge and allow you to identify their misconceptions. However, remember that whatever time you give to this teaching, students will appreciate written guidance and clear regulations for use later. They may also appreciate signposting to sites such as those listed on page 91.

Detection

6

Detecting and dealing with plagiarism will always be a less attractive option than designing out opportunities and teaching students the skills they need to comply with academic conventions. However, it is likely that, intentionally or unintentionally, students will plagiarise. When that happens, individuals need to act to ensure the integrity of their own institutions' awards and of higher education in general.

Reactive detection is a three step process: first, your suspicion is aroused then, upon further investigation, a case emerges and subsequent investigation leads to either a decision to continue the case under a disciplinary process or a decision that no academic misconduct has occurred. This is a relatively familiar process that academics have followed with greater or lesser enthusiasm for years. Proactive detection, on the other hand, is a relatively recent phenomenon, offering the possibility of screening students' work rather than waiting for an individual case to crop up. This chapter looks at all of these aspects – suspicion, confirmation and screening – and suggests how you might improve your ability to spot and confirm plagiarism.

Think about:

- what currently alerts you to possible plagiarism?

- what do you currently ignore (in student work) even though it might be plagiarism and if you do so, why?

- what would you never ignore and why?

A threat from over-detection?

It is tempting (and apparently fitting) to believe that a problem greatly aided by the development of communication and information technology (C&IT) can best be dealt with by means of that self-same C&IT. However, there is clear evidence that such an approach is ultimately self-defeating. Cole and Kiss (2000) describe the use of surveillance cameras, silent pagers, and tiny video cameras by cheaters in American universities, which in turn leads to lecturers using forensic linguistics to catch them. They call this behaviour a 'dispiriting arms race ... reminiscent of James Bond' (p. 6). In fact, like any purely 'catch-and-punish' approach (only more so), it will simply lead to a never-ending 'arms-race' between the students and the university.

Under-reporting of plagiarism

> ### Think about:
>
> * whose job do you believe detection to be?
>
> * what might the long-term consequences be of significant under-detection for your course? For your students? For you?

Anecdotal evidence suggests that some or possibly even many academics avoid detection if at all possible. It is difficult to see how else one can explain the wide disparity between the incidents of plagiarism acted upon by staff and those reported anecdotally and in the literature by the students themselves (see, for example, the statistics cited in Chapter 1). Clearly, one reason for under-reporting by academic staff is simply lack of time. Evidence of the significant increase in workload for all staff in higher education over the last 10 years or more is so widespread as not to need citation. But although pressure on time is a key deterrent, other academic worries also contribute to their reluctance to act.

Some staff cite an absence of clear teaching on how to avoid plagiarism and see detection as unfair on students generally and potentially discriminatory against international students. For others, pointing the finger of blame at some students is viewed as unfair if other students, taught by other staff, are not equally at risk. Some staff may believe that they would be seen as having failed as teachers compared with other staff who had not discovered extensive plagiarism amongst their students (even if lack of detection in the latter case arises from those colleagues not having looked). Finally, I have heard many staff complain bitterly that their management does not back their wish to pursue a case against a student for plagiarism. Instead of support, these academics claim their managers were more worried about the school or university appearing on the front page of the THES in a less than flattering light or losing the revenue of a student facing dismissal. Comments in Chapter 8 on institutional policies and culture may go some way in addressing all these worries though none of the approaches suggested in this handbook will banish such matters completely.

If you try too hard, all you catch is the clumsy ones and the students will spend more time outwitting you than learning.

A UK lecturer

This chapter takes the view that all plagiarism should be dealt with and that individual academics need the skills, time and support necessary to do this job well. A lecturer who sees plagiarism and does not take action might be contributing to the alleged diminution of academic values that often features in the national press and will certainly be letting down honest students who made an effort to produce the work in question.

Think about:

- does your willingness to take action or ignore plagiarism have an impact on your students' motivation to learn?

- if you currently take a relatively relaxed approach to plagiarism, what might influence you to adopt a different approach?

Signs of plagiarism

Many academics are confident they can detect plagiarism. Most do so through paying attention to the student's writing style. In a survey of 321 academics, 67% of those surveyed said that terminology and sentence structure were significant, with 72% citing changes within the text as indicative. 63% were suspicious if the writing deviated from the student's expected level and 66% said they looked for 'a feeling of familiarity with the text' (Bull et al, 2001). Hinchliffe (1998) suggests some clues are even more obvious, not to say blatant, such as:

- urls left at the top of students' pages;

- strange changes in font and/or layout;

- American spelling either throughout a document or in scattered sections;

- bibliographies that only cite material not available locally;

- bibliographic references from 1996 and before (for example) in a paper on a topical issue;

- bibliographies that do not reflect the content of the coursework;

- introductions and conclusions written in grammatically incorrect English and not addressing the body of the paper that is written in flawless, complex English; and

- unusual or highly specific professional jargon in a student starting out in the discipline.

Colleagues who plagiarise

Teachers need to take their responsibilities as guardians of integrity more seriously. Research indicates that many avoid confronting [fellow academic] plagiarists. They may fear retaliation or they have witnessed cases where the system has suppressed investigation, discouraged 'negative publicity' and minimised academic misconduct. Why should they risk their careers if no one else cares? ... Safe ways of reporting and handling plagiarism claims need to be established since most fall into the grey area between a gentleman's agreement and an acrimonious lawsuit.

Wilfried Decoo, author of Crisis on Campus: confronting academic misconduct (MIT press, 2002) quoted in THES 22 Feb 2002.

Less blatant examples in written work should also make the reader uneasy. For example, coursework that:

- addresses the topic only obliquely or addresses only a small aspect of it

- is out of character for this particular student, especially if it significantly exceeds the usual level of performance or language

- closely resembles work submitted by other students.

Further suggestions of what to watch for

Harris (2001, page 63) suggests clues such as those cited above and adds suggestions about looking for:

- mixed bibliographies where two or more citation systems are used;

- 'lack of citations or quotations' in a long piece of prose; and

- 'signs of datedness' such as using statistics from a fixed and far off time frame or references to past events as if they were current – for example, an essay that purports to be contemporary might include a phrase about '…the good work being done by Mother Teresa'.

Some clues are useful only as a very preliminary trigger for further investigation. For example, Harris (p. 70) recommends looking at the length of sentences in different parts of the document:

> Software analysis of student essays shows that college freshmen usually have an average sentence length of about 15 to 17 words … As writers improve, sentence structures tend to grow more complex and hence sentence lengths increase. (Note that there are exceptions such as business prose and journalese, which set short sentences as a goal.) Generally, however, if the sentences of an entire paper or a section of a paper are unusually long [or if] sentences vary in average length [with some paragraphs] featuring sentences of an average of 15 words while others have 28 word sentences … you may want to give the paper a second look for copying.

Remember that sentence length and complexity can vary greatly in many people's writing. This and other characteristics can occur in work genuinely constructed by the student and are only indications of the need for further investigation, not conclusive in themselves.

Choosing the right detection tool

Note: It is likely that changes and developments in this area will accelerate as interest in their use grows. Therefore any comments here will need checking in the light of the most recent advice available. In early 2002, the Joint Information Systems Committee launched a major project on electronic detection of plagiarism and began setting up a centre charged with disseminating good practice in its use. See http://www.jisc.ac.uk/plagiarism for information on this initiative.

Using electronic detection

You will need to decide whether you will operate reactively, investigating individual students or proactively, screening all work. Some institutions adopt a middle ground, spot-checking only some work.

Whatever you decide, you will need to inform students, secure the resources needed and keep in step with colleagues who may be doing the same. This is likely to become easier if national initiatives begin to identify and promulgate good practice in this area. You need to start by choosing an appropriate electronic detection tool.

Tools for detecting collusion

If you are worried about students copying from each other rather than from an outside source such as books or the Web, you need a tool that checks for overlap between different scripts such as CopyCatch, devised by a forensic linguist and available for purchase (see resources page 89). To use CopyCatch, you load student's word-processed scripts, usually in text format, into the programme which then requires a relatively short time to match each script with all the others in the cohort. The designers claim that matches over 60% or 70% (depending on the task) are clear indications of the need for specific checking of those papers more closely. The tool can also provide information that would not otherwise be available. For example, it could spot significant overlap in two pieces of work in a large cohort where an individual marker might not notice similarities or where multiple markers would be unaware of similar scripts. As with all detection tools, any finding requires a subsequent judgement as to whether academic misconduct has occurred and what further action needs to be taken, if any.

Another way to check for collusion is to use a commercial site such as Turnitin.com (described below). This product will both search the Web for similar text and review previously submitted student work. A 2001 study of Turnitin's effectiveness noted that, over time, this aspect of building a bespoke database could become a significant aid to plagiarism detection (Bull et al, 2001).

Tools for detecting the use of Web-based material

If you wish to check a single case, powerful search engines such a Google will compare an uploaded paragraph or even locate a five- or six-word phrase, placing the phrase you wish to find in "double quotes". (You must, of course, choose a phrase which is unusual or significant.) In my experience, using Google is by far the most common way lecturers deal with one-off cases and check whether further investigation is warranted. Google searches can be enhanced by using the similar pages function following each citation, which will bring up a list of the sites that are related to your first result. More results from the same site may be signalled and could be useful as guidance for further checking. However, even though Google itself is fast and produces a ranked list as to relevance, searching this way can take time (sometimes up to several hours), and depends on your ability to navigate the Web.

Another way to check a single example of student writing is to ask several search engines to look for the same five or six-word phrase, thereby increasing the range of your search. Harris (2001), explores detection in some detail in his book, *The Plagiarism Handbook,* offering extensive advice and resources. He reminds the reader that:

> ... no search engine covers more than about a third of the visible web (even the engines indexing more than a billion pages), so you could try several ... Google, Northern Light, Fast, AltaVista, HotBot and Lycos would be one sample set (p. 76).

Or you could employ a meta-search tool such as Mamma (http://www.mamma.com) which functions by searching other search engines.

Commercially available detection tools are an alternative to searching yourself for the source of suspected plagiarsism arising from the Web. Some of these products search the Web with a programme under your control such as the Essay Verification Engine or EVE (http://canexus.com/eve/index.shtml); others ask you to submit work and provide a report of possible sources, sometimes immediately but more commonly within 24 hours as, for example, Turnitin does. Views on the utility or otherwise of these packages vary. Bull et al (2001) provided a Which-style review of five electronic detection tools and concluded they do provide a useful service but confirmed the concerns listed below. (See also page 91 for a list of electronic detection sites.)

Tools for investigating whether the student was the author

The Glatt Plagiarism Screening Program claims to diagnose a student's 'individual style of writing' which is 'as unique as fingerprints'. (http://www.plagiarism.com/INDEX.HTM) The site's publicity material claims it:

> ... eliminates every fifth word of the suspected student's paper and replaces the words with a standard size blank. The student is asked to supply the missing words. The number of correct responses, the amount of time intervening, and various other factors are considered in assessing the final Plagiarism Probability Score.

The designers claim no false accusations have been made but Culwin and Lancaster (2001, p. 7), after reviewing many electronic detection tools, comment, 'it is unclear how much trust could be placed in the results'. I 'failed' the sample test when asked to reproduce words 'eliminated from' text that I had previously written. You can try the system yourself on their Web site in a small task. The developers claim Glatt is especially useful in cases where the original cannot be located.

Plagiarism in computing source code

Culwin et al (2001) reviewed a range of products designed to detect plagiarism in source code, that is in the code that underpins computer programmes (see http://www.jisc.ac.uk/pub01/southbank.pdf). The authors conclude that two commercially available packages – JPlag and MOSS (see page 91 for urls) – are effective in detecting plagiarism but are not widely used. A survey conducted at the same time as the product review pointed to much higher levels of plagiarism than are currently being dealt with officially, leading to the authors concluding that many more computing departments could usefully screen students' work using these tools. They also note that some departments have developed their own in-house detection tools.

Think about:

- if you were to start using electronic detection, what would be the first step?

- who might be interested in working with you in this initiative?

Issues in using electronic detection tools

A balanced, realistic assessment of the role of electronic detection is likely to take time but as more and more institutions adopt them, good practice guidelines will emerge. In the meantime, you will need to consider the following issues:

- **scope** – Hinchliffe (2000) notes that detection tools can only access the relatively small percentage of the Internet that is indexed on search engines. Copyright rules and protection devices mean that much of the Web is only available to subscribers or members. Many essay banks only offer a small sample of work such as the first paragraph unless you provide your credit card details.

- **reliability** – any detection tool reliant on the Web will be subject to all the vagaries of that medium. Bull et al (2001) tested five tools over two months and found they had different results at different times depending on which sites were active.

- **detecting fraud** – detection tools cannot identify the author of a piece of work. If a student pays someone, uses one of the free essay banks then disguises cleverly, or translates work from one language into another, this will be undetected.

- **overlooking print sources** – Hinchliffe (2000, p. 6) notes:

  > ... the savvy, intentional plagiariser will use older periodical articles or, even more difficult to track though not impossible, book chapters. Tracking these original source documents requires expertise in identifying clues in the original texts and then retrieving those print documents.

- **copyright and data protection issues** – some institutions worry that because coursework belongs to the student, they cannot do anything without explicit student permission (often seen as a huge administrative headache). Others see it differently and simply inform students that checks will be made, taking the view that they have a duty to verify the originality of student work. Some detection tools offer as a feature the avoidance of copyright issues as the document *per se* is not involved as it is encoded for detection purposes.

One data-protection manager's views

The Data Protection Act is relevant because it governs how you process personal information which in this case, will be the link between a named student and a particular mark or comment offered in feedback. Asking for consent to store the work is pointless, would any student refuse? If they want their degree then coursework is non optional, though I suggest that it is made clear to them when the assignment is set that this is what will be done, and why you want to do it (especially the plagiarism check). You also need to tell them if you will share their information with anyone outside the university. Who knows there might be someone who then decides not to submit their work!

Once you have [students'] personal information you must make arrangements to keep it securely to prevent unauthorized access, amendment, or loss. Once you've finished with the information you must dispose of it securely, making sure that all copies are deleted.

If you automatically scan the student's text, the Data Protection Act states that 'no decision must be taken that significantly affects the individual that is based solely on processing by automatic means'. The target for the DPA is things like 'credit scoring' where a computer is not allowed to make the final decision but would also apply here.

Carroll, personal communication, 2002

Another concern is **the effect of using electronic detection on the learning environment**. Evidence of the effect remains anecdotal. A study conducted in 2000 in five British institutions of higher education was designed to investigate the use of electronic detection (Chester, 2001). It reported the majority of students were 'hostile' and 'expressed considerable concern', in one instance only agreeing to participate in the study if 'they were assured that plagiarism identified by the system would not be penalised'. Freewood (2001) interviewed students who saw detection as Big Brother tactics although most were pleased that action was being taken against cheaters.

Staff development and training

Some lecturers need help in learning to use the more complex detection tools and most appreciate a chance to share expertise and pool good practice. Usually, the more technologically minded people lead the way, with the less keen adopting things more slowly. Because, in general,

'The Web's plagiarism police'

... as educators begin to rely more on technology, hopefully they'll realise that – at least for now – nothing can completely replace the watchful eyes of human beings ... I put a friend's research paper in the system [a commercially available Web searching tool] ... and it found five phrases that matched other sources found on the Net. The report said 'the paper probably contains plagiarised material'...but a quick check showed that the indicted [sic] sentences were all legitimate excerpts, appearing within quotation marks and citing sources ... the service came across like a hanging judge.

http://www.salon.com/tech/feature/1999/06/14/plagiarism/index.html

academics seem most willing to learn from colleagues within their own institution, training programmes based on networking with enthusiasts and discussion linked to one-to-one coaching where necessary will probably be the most effective. It is important that this pragmatic, incremental approach happens alongside measures for institution-wide monitoring of practice, decisions and punishments (see Chapter 8). Students will expect a common approach, despite the inevitable different rates of progress.

Academic decisions, not electronic decisions

Making a judgement about plagiarism is in many ways no different from marking a paper. In both cases, your conclusion will be based on your own experience and skill. Of course, as Chapter 8 describes, students are empowered to challenge decisions about plagiarism under disciplinary procedures whereas they are not allowed to question grades and marks. The consequences of an accusation of plagiarism on the student can also be more significant, as set out on pages 74 and 75. It follows therefore that you will need to be able to defend your accusation robustly and there are several ways you might do so.

The strongest defence is to find the original source, but this is not a necessary component of a strong case for plagiarism. This is civil law where the balance of probabilities is the standard of proof, rather than 'beyond reasonable doubt' as in criminal law. You could show a piece of work is, on balance, unlikely to be the student's own if any or all of these are demonstrated, even if you did not find the source:

- there is a marked contrast between the style, fluency and level of language used by the student in observed writing and in the presented work;

- an oral viva reveals marked unfamiliarity with the contents and underlying concepts covered by the work (see page 38);

- there are any of the examples of blatant plagiarism listed at the head of this chapter;

- evidence gained from discussion with the student (see below) further confirms the view that the work is not the student's own.

Discussing a possible case of plagiarism with a student

> **Think about:**
> - what does your institution stipulate you must do when interviewing a student?
> - what actions would be sensible prior to asking a student to attend an interview?

(See Chapter 8 for issues relating to institutional responsibilities and operating within institutional guidelines.)

Culwin and Lancaster (2001) make a useful distinction between verification, checking that something is not acceptable, and investigation where the student has to be shown the evidence of plagiarism and given the opportunity to explain it. By the time most academics talk to students about an alleged case of plagiarism, they are probably investigating rather than verifying. Before you speak to a student, you need to be clear what the purpose of the discussion might be. A viva for the purpose of assessing the student's knowledge, as described on page 38, is a way of checking authenticity for all students, not plagiarism in a few. It could also serve as a deterrent, encouraging students to put the work in because they might be questioned. However, what began as assessment could become investigation if you become concerned that the work being assessed is not the student's own. If the interview shifts from verifying to investigating, ensure both you and the student are aware of the change of purpose of the interview. The rest of this section deals with investigative interviews.

Harris notes (2001, pp. 83-4), 'Emotionally charged meetings need clear structure if they are to maintain orderliness and a sense of objectivity. The value of knowing the rules and having a plan cannot be overestimated.' He also cautions, 'Remember you may be wrong' and reminds the reader, 'therefore treat all students with respect.'

When interviewing a student under investigation, careful open questioning is likely to be the most productive. You might start by calmly inviting student comment using phrases like, 'I have read your recent report and have some concerns. Can you tell me about how you went about writing it?' If you are unsure and wish to verify your suspicions, ask about the content of the document and the process the student followed in writing it. Engage the student in discussion about their sources, asking perhaps where they looked, when they did so, what

I put all the student work through CopyCatch [see page 65 above] and two came out as similar. But when I looked, it was obvious they had not colluded. Yes, they had some of the same things but they had written very different papers. Also, the quotes they used were properly referenced.

A UK lecturer

they found and how they used specific resources mentioned. You might also discuss in more depth any source that was particularly central to the argument. If you notice that the student has difficulty with technical or unusual words, ask for definitions.

If the case has already been verified and the interview has the primary purpose of investigating the case, you could start by providing the student with a copy of the academic regulations relevant to plagiarism, reading the section or sections aloud and asking if the student has any comment. When a student is interviewed in my institution, where plagiarism is dealt with by an experienced and senior person who holds a position entitled 'Academic Misconduct Officer', the student is already aware that a case has been alleged and that the interview is designed to explore the issues and consider and possibly impose penalties. It nevertheless starts as an investigation.

There are a growing number of institutions reporting that students who know they are attending an investigative interview insist on bringing a solicitor. Anecdotal reports of solicitors' adversarial and aggressive manner are growing. Academics describe demands for proof and threats of dire consequences where allegations are not upheld, leaving them (the academics) feeling intimidated and worried. As investigative interviews usually precede disciplinary cases, serving to gather evidence to prepare a case rather than putting one for challenge as described in Chapter 8, legal representation seems inappropriate. Your institution may already have guidance on who may be considered as an appropriate companion or supporter for a student in such an interview. Certainly advice should be sought should a student seek legal support at this stage.

However you approach the interview, expect students to treat the discussion as significant and highly charged, so be careful not to interpret understandable signs of nervousness as indicative of their possible guilt. In general, such interviews last about 40 to 60 minutes and will require careful notes recording what was discussed and the outcomes.

See Chapter 8 for a discussion of ways in which institutions might handle detection other than by asking individual lecturers to undertake the investigation.

Punishment

7

Once plagiarism has been detected, investigated and confirmed, it is important that the student is punished fairly, consistently and in accordance with the principles of natural justice. The next chapter offers suggestions about how institutional frameworks and procedures must underpin punishment decisions. This chapter covers how to guard against unfairness, suggests methods you might use in assigning a tariff to an individual student's plagiarism, and recommends that you inform students as a whole of actions taken against the minority who do not follow academic regulations.

Fairness

The UK Quality Assurance Agency (QAA) has charged institutions to have 'effective mechanisms to deal with breaches of assessment regulations' (QAA Code of Practice on Assessment, 2000, Precept 3) and to conduct assessment 'with rigour and fairness and with due regard for security' (op cit., Precept 5). Moreover, it is certainly arguable that Article 6 of the European Convention of Human Rights now applies (via the Human Rights Act) to university disciplinary procedures (and because these assumptions must be tested via cases, which institution wants to be the first to test this belief in the courts?).

In this context, a fair procedure is one that adheres to the principles of natural justice, produces outcomes proportionate to the magnitude of the offence, and one that is consistently applied across the whole university. Fair procedures would:

- require that a student be presented with all the evidence;

- give the student an opportunity to challenge the evidence in front of the body that will determine the punishment;

- provide all participants in the process with appropriate notice;

- offer students information on their rights including representation by 'an appropriately skilled and qualified person, particularly in serious or complex cases' (Carroll and Appleton, 2001); and advise students how evidence can be challenged – as this is a civil matter, the 'balance of probabilities' is the criteria for proof; Hart (2001) reminds higher education institutions that:

> … it is generally accepted that the criminal standard [of proof] is too strict for internal disciplinary proceedings. However, it is also considered that the more serious the charge, the more satisfied the committee needs to be that the offence has been committed.

In addition to being a requirement of natural justice, the process of debating and testing the evidence of plagiarism is also a key opportunity to reinforce the definitions and examples of what constitutes acceptable and unacceptable academic citation, paraphrasing, etc. Certainly when I interview academics who conduct disciplinary cases involving plagiarism, they seem convinced that the experience is a powerful learning opportunity for the student or students involved.

Determining appropriate punishments

It is not possible, in my view, to offer strict guidelines or suggest predetermined penalties for plagiarism – circumstances vary too much – although some are suggested (see page 77 for one example). However, it is possible to reach consensus on the factors to consider when setting punishments and the relative importance of each in making the decision, seeking consistency but not conformity. My own institution uses the following four factors in determining punishment.

1. The extent of the academic misconduct

In my experience, this is the first factor mentioned by academics seeking to set a penalty for plagiarism, regardless of the other factors listed below. They determine extent by looking at such things as the amount of text plagiarised, the closeness to the original text, the nature of the material copied, and whether copied material was purely descriptive or included results.

2. The student's intention or motivation

Not intending plagiarism does not exonerate the student – plagiarism is plagiarism. But the converse, clearly **intending** plagiarism (and this is often hard to show), might be grounds for awarding an increased punishment. This factor seems especially important towards the beginning of a student's programme (see below). If the student intended to gain an unfair advantage via fraud or was grossly negligent in not taking sufficient steps to prevent themselves from committing

[A student commented that] receiving a warning in the first year for relying too heavily on set text material from the tutor acted to legitimise the use of his [the student who was warned] own personal voice. Through the warning he not only went away to learn how to reference properly so he would not get 'caught out' again but also came to a better understanding of how to use secondary sources and be original in the way of looking at them. [The student] concluded by saying that he now not only gets better marks but finds that the tutors appreciate the value of his work, too.

Freewood (2001, p. 4).

plagiarism, they have committed a further offence. However, some institutions stipulate that an instance of plagiarism may not be treated as minor unless the student admits to intending to plagiarise with major cases involving the full disciplinary procedure. This is probably unacceptable as it smacks of coercion. The distinction between so-called major and minor plagiarism must be made by academic staff using, I would suggest, these factors which can be assumed to impact on the student's actions and motivation:

- **the stage of the student in their programme** – most institutions are less punitive in the early stages though for reasons outlined in Chapter 4, all cases should be noted and care should be taken that the student does less well than if no plagiarism had been identified;

- **the number of previous offences** (note: many institutions do not keep sufficient records to use this factor but for the reasons stated at the start of this chapter, should now be doing so); and

- **the learning background of the student** – how familiar might this student be with UK conventions, academic writing or the rules of the discipline? What can be assumed about the extent of the student's knowledge of the concept of academic misconduct and by extension, professional misconduct?

3. The conventions in the academic field or discipline

Students need to be judged within the relevant disciplinary conventions. If they are working across disciplines, they need to be informed of the rules within which they are currently active. Biologists and historians, for example, may hold very different views about the importance of citation, attribution and crediting others' work.

4. The effect of the intended penalty on the student's progression or (potential) award

The overall outcome should not be disproportionate to the offence. In different programmes, the same decision may have very different effects, for example, delaying the student's progression for 12 months in one case and only conferring a lower mark in another. A more significant impact might be the consequences of a charge of misconduct on a student's future professional status. Students who are guilty of not abiding by academic conventions by, for example, misusing the finer points of citation have plagiarised but need to be distinguished from students who have committed fraud (e.g. by downloading a completed essay off the Web or copying a fellow student's paper, changing only the title page and name). The former offence is probably only significant within academia whereas the latter is universally seen as cheating. If your institution does not make such distinctions, you will need to seek advice before allocating punishments that evoke a full disciplinary process for all plagiarism. It would not be just to deny someone the right to be a nurse, a social worker or to practise law, for example, because of a minor violation of referencing conventions which automatically becomes a charge of misconduct. In the three examples above, you may be obliged to report the misconduct to the appropriate professional licensing body, which may, in turn, see misconduct as a potential grounds for refusing a licence to practise.

Consistency

Over time, applying the above factors to specific cases and sharing views on what constitutes major and minor plagiarism will lead to an agreed system of 'tariffs'. These are not static or closed decisions; rather they need to be 'alive', public and visible. Unfortunately, this is rarely the case. Walker (1998) surveyed academic staff in New Zealand and found that although plagiarism was 'fairly commonplace within the faculty in question', staff showed a 'lack of awareness of institutional policies … anomalies in those policies, inconsistencies in the way that [they] appear to be responding'. The study was limited in scale but its findings are consistent with the literature elsewhere. Walker's call for 'guidelines, procedures and penalties … [that] would go some way towards establishing an atmosphere of openness and trust between university [managers] and academic staff' (p. 103) continues to be relevant. In my experience, moving from being able to say 'yes, I guess we have a plagiarism policy' to ensuring that policy is alive, followed and understood can take several years, even where the institution is actively pushing its widespread use. In the meantime, access to specialists and visible monitoring of decisions will be particularly important for academics seeking to implement the policy. The next chapter suggests how this might be achieved.

Think about:

- what punishments are applied in your own university? In your school or department? For your own students?

- how were they determined and by whom?

- are they widely known or public?

Suggested procedures and penalties for plagiarism

Plagiarism type	Procedure	Penalty
Sham paraphrasing	Academic staff member brings to attention of student	**Minor:** marks deducted equal to 10-50% of assignment value, depending on amount, no resubmission permitted **Major:** marks deducted equal to 10-100% of assignment value depending on amount, no resubmission permitted
Illicit paraphrasing	Academic staff member officially censures student, copy of letter to HoD and dean of faculty	**Minor:** marks deducted equal to 10-50% of assignment value, depending on amount, no resubmission permitted **Major:** marks deducted equal to 51-100% of assignment value, depending on amount, no resubmission permitted
Other plagiarism type one: both students currently in course	Students interviewed by HoD and officially censured in writing. Copy of letter to dean of faculty	**Minor:** original assignment marked and assessed at no more than 50%, copy assignment marked and assessed at no more than 25% **Major:** original assignment marked and assessed at no more than 50%, copy assignment rated 0%
Other plagiarism type two: one student completed course previously	Students interviewed by HoD and officially censured in writing. Copy of letter to dean of faculty	**Minor:** copy assignment marked and assessed at no more than 25%; course credit of colluding student reviewed **Major:** copy assignment rated 0%; course credit of colluding student reviewed
Verbatim copying	Student interviewed by HoD and officially censured in writing. Copy of letter to dean of faculty	**Minor:** assignment marked and assessed at no more than 25% of total marks **Major:** assignment assessed at 0%, no resubmission permitted
Recycling	Student brought before dean/disciplinary committee; entry in official record	Assignment rated 0%; student placed on probation for rest of period of study
Ghost writing	Student brought before dean/disciplinary committee; entry in official record	Assignment rated 0%, student placed on probation for rest of period of study
Purloining	Student brought before dean/disciplinary committee; entry in official record	Assignment rated 0% and/or course credit withdrawn depending on seriousness of offence

Source: J. Walker, *Higher Education Research and Development*, Vol. 17, No. 1, 1998, pp. 89-106 (reproduced with permission from TaylorFrancis Ltd. http://www.tandf.co.uk/journals)

A case study in setting and agreeing tariffs

I reviewed one institution's sanctions over 12 months and found the following were used, listed in ascending order of severity (Carroll, 2002, unpublished). Some sanctions were used frequently, others rarely and some were not fully compliant with institutional regulations, a finding that could probably be replicated in many UK universities. My enquiries revealed these penalties

1. discussion with the course teacher leading to resubmission of the plagiarised work for full marks, no record kept;

2. discussion with the module leader, record kept, resubmission of the same work for full marks;

3. discussion with a specialist disciplinary officer, no record kept, no penalty;

4. discussion with a specialist disciplinary officer, record kept, no penalty;

[All further actions result from discussions with a specialist disciplinary officer (e.g. Dean, Head of Department etc.) and all were recorded]

5. resubmission of a different task/new work for full marks;

6. re-marking of the original work with plagiarised section removed, mark reflects remaining work;

7. resubmission of new work for a reduced mark (e.g. 10% reduction);

8. resubmission of new work for a minimal passing mark;

9. zero for the piece of work, no resubmission;

10. zero grade for the module;

11. failure of the programme;

12. removal from the programme or university.

In discussion with academics who, between them, had dealt with more than 150 cases, it seemed clear that they considered actions 1–4 as appropriate if two or more of the following criteria was present:

- a small amount of the work was involved or plagiarism occurred in a part of the work of lesser importance (eg appendices);

- it was early in the student's academic career;

- there is well-founded reason to suppose the student did not understand academic conventions;

- the plagiarism arose solely from misuse of academic conventions and not from fraud.

Several mentioned sanction number 4 [the interview with the disciplinary officer] as a significant deterrent and saw it as effective for the student concerned and for the cohort as 'the word got around'. Sanctions 5, 6 and 7 were used when only one of the above criteria was present or when the extent of the plagiarism could not be considered 'small'. The extent of the plagiarism on its own was sufficient to invoke the more stringent actions. Several pointed out that sanction number 5 can be a considerable punishment for hard-pressed students.

Sanction number 8 (resubmission of new work for a minimal grade) was used most widely and most frequently. It was considered appropriate where the student:

- plagiarised sufficiently to render the work un-markable if the offending extract or extracts was/were removed;

- could be assumed to understand UK academic conventions; or

- lifted a relatively small amount of work without alteration or attribution [note: if this was a significant amount of the total coursework, actions 10 and 11 were more common].

Sanction 12, [removal from the programme or the university] was only used after repeated, fraudulent and serious plagiarism but in this particular university, it was used.

> **Think about:**
>
> - how consistent is punishment in your institution?
>
> - if you wished to adopt a system of shared tariffs to increase institutional consistency, where might you start?
>
> - how could you inform students of this change?

Publicising punishment decisions

Punishments can be used to inform and teach an individual student but will only be effective for students as a whole if disciplinary actions are made public without, of course, reverting to 'name and shame' tactics. Publication could also counter the more fanciful messages that circulate on the informal grapevine when measures to tackle plagiarism are introduced. Your own institution will probably offer several channels such as student representatives, a regular column in the student newspaper, or specific mention at induction sessions. Wherever you give the message, take care to balance it with measures that involve students and value their learning. Without that balance, students might over-react, assuming perhaps that you are running a 'catch and punish' programme or, if numbers are small, that statistics imply permission to transgress with impunity.

Impact of punishment on others

Fear of punishment was cited as the best deterrence in one study of 11 undergraduates, yet none of the students questioned was able to tell the interviewer what the punishments were. Where they could cite examples of friends being disciplined, they did not know what actually happened to them. The researcher commented that, 'if plagiarism is seen to be occurring and either remains undetected or unpunished students can feel despondent about the value that is put on their individual work or their course in general. It also acts to tempt them into considering plagiarism because they think they will get away with it and do not see why they should do the work if others are not.'

Freewood (2001, p. 7)

Institutional policy and culture

8

Much of the thinking and most of the ideas in this section arise from work with my colleague, Jon Appleton and were previously published in Plagiarism: a Good Practice Guide on http://www.jisc.ac.uk/pub01/brookes.pdf (Carroll and Appleton, 2001).

Elsewhere in this handbook, actions by individuals and groups are discussed. In this chapter, the focus shifts to the institution where a number of policies and practices must be in place to underpin and work with the individual's actions. If you are tackling plagiarism yourself, start by checking whether your institution's procedures include:

- a clear separation between the assessment and disciplinary processes;

- a clear, fair and consistent disciplinary procedure;

- widely disseminated information about how the institution values learning and tackles plagiarism; and

- a statement specifying staff responsibilities in relation to each point above.

If they do not, it will be more difficult to make your individual actions effective and ensure they are fair to students.

Think about:

- does your institution treat students fairly?

- if it doesn't, what might help?

- does your institution make it possible for you to do even some of the actions described elsewhere in this handbook?

- if it doesn't, how might the institution be encouraged to provide you the help and support you need to tackle plagiarism?

- what's the first step?

Adopting a disciplinary approach

In the past, academics handled plagiarism as and when they found it, often (but not always) following institutional procedures. They investigated, confirmed plagiarism and imposed punishments. This had much to commend it – it was relatively fast, could accommodate information and circumstances known to the teacher, and offered the option of 'creative' solutions ('You two colluded, the work is worth 60 marks. You can each have 30; now go away.'). Over time, ad hoc tariffs were developed that punished students but did not jeopardise their future, academic or otherwise. However, changing circumstances and external requirements make this kind of approach unacceptable (if, in fact, it ever was). Asking each academic to deal with plagiarism means most have little knowledge of procedures (Walker, 1998) and encounter few cases. Thus, they are likely to apply procedures inconsistently, keep few records and (inadvertently) deny students their rights (see below).

Individual handling also means the cost of pursuing a case rests with the person who spots it. I have often heard academics describe the sinking feeling one gets when reading through a script and the thought, 'This is plagiarised' grows ever stronger. Do you award a lower mark and ignore it or blow the whistle and face hours, perhaps even days, of work?

A new approach is needed. **All plagiarism must now be dealt with through a formal process and all punishments must conform to disciplinary regulations.** Reasons for this are given at the beginning of this chapter and further elaborated below. This seemingly hard-and-fast rule may seem too severe or even an over-reaction but there are ways to ensure that cases can be handled with some speed (see the section on 'fast tracking' below) and ways to lift the burden from the individual (see below on academic misconduct officers).

Using a separate procedure for disciplinary issues

One value of the disciplinary procedure is that it clearly separates procedures for examination from those for dealing with misconduct. Put crudely, an examination board considers the extent to which a piece of work demonstrates that the student has achieved the necessary learning outcomes and determines what academic credit should be awarded for it. Examination boards apply procedures developed through internal quality assurance and external peer review via external examiners, for example.

A disciplinary committee, on the other hand, will consider whether or not the evidence presented to it is sufficient to warrant a finding of academic misconduct and, if so, what penalty should be imposed. Some

The Sydney Morning Herald, 24 February 2001, printed a story headlined 'The case of a student who got away with Net plagiarism scot-free'. It described an Australian case which appeared to show beyond doubt that a student downloaded two essays off the Web. The Vice Chancellor of the university concerned commented, 'allegations that the … student had cheated might be true but staff who tried to fail the student had not followed correct procedures.' The student graduated with a degree.

penalties, such as expulsion from the university, go beyond the normal powers of examination boards and many could be imposed without reference to the merits or otherwise of the (non-plagiarised) remainder of the work submitted. Unlike assessment procedures, those for disciplinary committees are governed by the rules of natural justice (and quite possibly now the Human Rights Act) (see Chapter 1). Moreover, once a disciplinary committee has made its decision a subsequent examination board must be extremely careful not to revisit or seek to alter the decisions made by that disciplinary committee.

The distinction between examination and discipline has been tested in the courts (Carroll and Appleton, 2001) and case law shows that when the processes of the two systems (assessment and discipline) are combined or mixed, this can lead to a successful challenge to the outcome. Thus, in R v Manchester Metropolitan University *ex parte* Nolan (1993), Mr Justice Sedley was clear that the exclusion of a student from the meeting of the examination board that considered an allegation of plagiarism against him was:

> … not beyond challenge if its effect were to rob a student altogether of a hearing by or on behalf of those who were to judge him, not – I stress – on examination performance but on the academic equivalent of a criminal charge (p. 21).

Please note that the use of the word 'criminal' in the above statement does not alter the fact that such cases are conducted under civil law. Mr Justice Sedley also confirmed that one process must accept the other's findings, stating 'it was the obligation of the board of examiners to accept and not to revise or go back on the findings of the disciplinary committee' when quashing the decision of an examination board to permanently fail a student for plagiarism (ibid. p. 22).

The requirements of natural justice

The principles of natural justice require that a student be presented with all the evidence, should an accusation of plagiarism be pursued, and be given an opportunity to challenge it in front of the body that will determine the punishment. All participants in the process should be given appropriate notice; and the student in particular should be told about his or her rights of representation by a skilled and qualified person. Building on the discussion on page 72, this might be a solicitor but need not necessarily be so. The student's right to challenge the evidence is particularly important in cases where it has not been possible to identify the original of the allegedly plagiarised material (see page 70).

Applying a penalty

Chapter 7 discussed at some length how penalties might be arrived at. Here, the matter is what happens when penalties are applied. Most judgements of plagiarism do not lead to the student's expulsion and the disciplinary committee must decide what punishment short of expulsion is justified. Failure of a piece of work or failure of a course unit can be dealt with by the examination committee in exactly the same way as for any other student with a similar record of failure, however caused.

Where a piece of work is judged suitable for some academic credit despite plagiarism, the disciplinary committee may ask the academic concerned to remove the work judged to have been included through misconduct and mark what remains – a concept some academics view as impossible but others claim they do routinely. The resulting mark is then offered to the examinations board in the same way as any other mark.

Appeals

Policies must specify which elements of any outcome can be appealed against through the appropriate provisions of the disciplinary procedure and which, if any, can be reviewed by means of an appeal against a decision of an examination board. None of these distinctions is impossible to establish, and many are not even particularly difficult, but it is not clear whether all institutions have yet adopted such an approach. Appeals must be reviewed by individuals not directly linked to those who made the initial decision(s).

Consistent and effective application of the procedures

Problems associated with under-reporting of plagiarism and inconsistency of punishment have been discussed above and on page 76. Some institutions seek to deal with these difficulties by locating 'plagiarism specialists' centrally, perhaps in a quality assurance department or linked to the academic registrar. This allows for maximum coherence, and encourages speedy adoption of policies. However, these specialists may have difficulty accommodating the disparate and often discipline-specific nature of plagiarism (see pages 11 and 75). Also, given the uneven timing of, for example, coursework submission dates they are unlikely to be kept fully occupied conducting disciplinary cases and it is not clear what else they might be doing.

Another solution is to refer all academic misconduct cases to one or two staff who work in each subject area. Thus, a school of 40 or 50 academics might have one or two specialists charged with pursuing cases of plagiarism alongside their other duties. This ensures that cases are dealt with by someone who understands the academic area in question (and quite possibly knows the student as well). Limiting the numbers makes consistent decision-making a realistic possibility, maximises the cost benefits of any formal training provided and ensures expertise is maintained through regular practice. It is worth noting that, while the holder of such a role certainly needs a thorough understanding of the relevant academic issues, there is no automatic requirement that he or she be a member of the academic staff. He or she will, however, need to have this particular responsibility included in any workload planning or time allocation – on average, each case takes about two hours to consider and conclude, once the academic who spotted the plagiarism has alerted the specialist and does not include the time required for collecting and documenting evidence.

Whatever the model adopted, whether placing responsibility at the centre with a small number of specialists, or devolving it to all academics, your institution will need to show they have:

- ways of discussing decisions made in diverse situations, either through face-to-face meetings in a devolved system or through information gathering in a centralised one;

- data on who is doing what that is shared and evaluated;

- changes in policy in response to monitoring and evaluation of current practice; and

- continued efforts to inform and update all staff on how to deal with these issues.

Ensuring procedures are workable

If procedures become too complex or slow, staff are deterred from using them. Minor and/or uncontested cases (and they are the majority) need to be dealt with under a 'fast-track' process. Fast tracking allows the student to acknowledge error and move on, while also ensuring that the appropriate penalty is imposed. Fast-tracking is different from the ad hoc processes described at the beginning of this chapter because it operates within shared assumptions, using agreed tariffs and according to institutional procedures. The specialist disciplinary officer or centrally-based administrator applies penalties on behalf of a full disciplinary body. For the student, it is rather like accepting and paying a fixed penalty speeding fine rather than disputing and using the full court procedures. A fast-track process must allow for a return to the full disciplinary review described in most institution's policies immediately a dispute arises. A colleague who often deals in these matters advises, 'Using fast-track procedures in the case of serious allegations should be done with the utmost care, if at all, regardless of the student's views and wishes.'

Agreeing tariffs

If your institution sets up a fast-track process, agreement on tariffs becomes even more important. See pages 74–79 in Chapter 7.

Keeping records of decisions

All cases should be recorded and reasons for decisions shared with students. There is growing evidence of legal requirements to do so (Hart, 2001) but more importantly, it creates yet a further opportunity for teaching students. Record keeping can contribute to institutional development by enabling more detailed monitoring of outcomes. You need to ensure that records have sufficient detail and are properly analysed. It will be useful to look for:

- inconsistencies in the application of the disciplinary procedure between academic areas;

- areas where teaching of correct attribution could be strengthened;

- groups of students that are particularly vulnerable to misunderstanding attribution conventions; and

- common errors in attribution.

Informing students of university activities against plagiarism

Issues relating to ensuring that students understand the institution's requirements were considered at some length in previous chapters. Here, the matter is how the institution checks this has happened as part of their quality assurance arrangements. Admittedly, this is difficult to do as many students are not interested until it happens to them. Publicising penalties might encourage student interest (see page 80), but whatever approach is adopted, students should never be given reason to believe that, because the lecturer has not told them that work will be checked, they can cheat with impunity. Similarly, students should know when the lecturer is taking active steps to check the authenticity of student work by electronic screening. Random or partial checks are a legitimate adjunct to normal academic judgement. Such actions must be explained with care or years of effort to create an atmosphere of collegial working between staff and students might be put at risk. It seems likely that the relative novelty of electronic detection means good practice about informing students is still developing.

Implementing a co-ordinated strategy against plagiarism

An institution needs an overall policy to make sure that, through working in alignment, it gains the benefits of synergy and ensures that all students encounter frequent and consistent messages about plagiarism. Every institution will have to address this issue in a way that is sensitive to its existing culture, but all should be based on an explicit policy that includes:

- **a clear commitment from the highest levels of the university.** This makes the statement that the issue is important and that it is necessary to devote appropriate resources to tackling it. It reassures those worried by the negative impact of any possible short-term bad publicity; and it strengthens the concept that all parts of the university will adopt a consistent approach to the problem.

- **a clear and appropriate regulatory framework for defining and dealing with academic misconduct.**

- **clearly defined roles and responsibilities.** Each member of staff, every school and faculty needs to know what is expected of them and what they can expect from others.

- **access to support and specialist advice.** Carrying out a balanced policy will necessitate support from specialists and experts in areas such as assessing electronic detection aids, course/assessment design, academic misconduct disciplinary procedures, and teaching academic writing skills. In order to develop expertise, these individuals will need time to research the relevant field, analyse information from a range of sources and produce (and regularly update) guidance appropriate to the institution. Once developed, this expertise will need to be actively disseminated as well as made available on request to individuals and groups. Many staff would also benefit from more general training and support in the same areas – institutions will need to make time available for these activities, both for those delivering and receiving them.

- **measures for embedding practice.** Tackling academic misconduct will always remain a reactive process unless institutions integrate their development of methods for tackling academic misconduct relating to course design, teaching and assessment into the existing and normal course review and quality assurance procedures. Of course, additional resources to encourage implementation in the early stages may be necessary.

- **targets and timetables.** Public statements about realistic targets and action plans for achieving them will significantly aid progress. However, in order to set realistic targets it is likely that there will have to be some initial research to establish the current extent and nature of academic misconduct. This will require resources.

- **a procedure for reviewing progress.** This needs to be done on a regular basis, and the various aspects of the policy amended as appropriate.

Whilst the above section sets out the necessary components for institutional progress, the speed of change may well depend upon the appearance of enthusiasts and champions. Such individuals cannot be compelled into existence but most institutions have people who are interested in plagiarism, in electronic detection and in teaching students the requisite skills. The skill of a committed senior management will lie in identifying, encouraging and supporting such individuals if and when they appear.

Resources

Locating electronic resources

All the urls listed below will be accessible via the Oxford Centre for Staff and Learning Development web site on:

http://www.brookes.ac.uk/services/ocsd/4_resource/plagiarism.html

We will endeavour to keep this resource up-to-date and even add new resources as we discover them. As always, sites listed here may have changed, disappeared or transmogrified. However, all were functional in July, 2002.

Other books on plagiarism

The Plagiarism Handbook, Robert Harris (2002), Los Angeles: Pyrczak Publishing, ISBN 1 884585 35 3

> Harris' book takes a similar approach to this publication. It is aimed at the American market and provides detailed information on electronic detection, especially on tracking down sources.

Academic Dishonesty: An Educator's Guide, Bernard E. Whitley Jr. and Patricia Keith-Spiegel (2002), Lawrence Erlbaum Associates

> The authors state, 'The goal of [this book] is to provide university faculty with a concise handbook covering the full spectrum of issues related to academic dishonesty' so it covers more than plagiarism and considers techniques for encouraging academic integrity.

Student Cheating and Plagiarism in the Internet Era: A Wake-up Call, Lathrop, A. and Foss, K. (2000), Englewood, CO: Libraries Unlimited, Inc.

> Gretchen Pearson whose web site is frequently recommended as a rich resource (see below) comments, 'This is the book that I wish were my web page! While it purports to be for [secondary school] teachers and librarians, it is equally useful for those in higher education. Every academic library should own a copy of this book.'

Articles available on line

'Anti-plagiarism strategies for research papers', Robert Harris, version date: March 7, 2002, available on:
http://www.virtualsalt.com/antiplag.htm

'Cheating 101: paper mills and you', Teaching Effectiveness Seminar, Coastal Carolina University, March 5, 1999 (updated March 3, 2000, revised March 26, 2001), available on:

http://www.coastal.edu/library/papermil.htm

> This systematic look at paper mills offers useful links to articles about users' reactions, then suggests how to locate paper mills, how to detect plagiarised papers, how to track down suspicious papers, and how to combat plagiarism.

General sites about plagiarism

http://plagiarism.phys.virginia.edu/home.html
A site at the University of Virginia managed by Louis Bloomfield, an academic with an interest in plagiarism. It offers free access to his own detection tool and links to a well-filtered list of other sites plus space for whistleblowers to report plagiarism cases.

http://www.academicintegrity.org/index.asp
The Centre for Academic Integrity provides a forum to 'identify, affirm, and promote the values of academic integrity among students, faculty, teachers and administrators.' It also commissions and reports research on student cheating and offers further services to members.

http://tlt.its.psu.edu/suggestions/cyberplag/
A comprehensive site managed by the University of Pennsylvania. It is regularly updated and provides useful links to other sites and to electronic detection services.

http://www.lemoyne.edu/library/plagiarism.htm
A site designed and maintained by Gretchen Pearson at LeMoyne College in the USA and originally created to support a seminar on managing information.

http://www.lib.utexas.edu/services/instruction/faculty/plagiarism/index.html
This site at the University of Texas is often cited by others who are setting up their own sites or investigating plagiarism.

Sites with an emphasis on teaching students about plagiarism

http://www.princeton.edu/pr/pub/integrity/pages/plagiarism.html Offers extensive guidance, information and examples.

http://education.indiana.edu/~frick/plagiarism/
Includes an online quiz with 10 items to demonstrate paraphrasing and citation rules that allows students to check their understanding.

http://www.library.ualberta.ca/guides/plagiarism/
A comprehensive site with information for teachers and students.

http://sja.ucdavis.edu/avoid.htm#guidelines
Offers guidelines and examples.

http://www.hamilton.edu/academic/Resource/WC/AvoidingPlagiarism.html
A frequently recommended site. Covers everything and offers good examples and exercises. Useful for generating handouts [with appropriate acknowledgement, of course].

Clarifying copyright

http://www.templetons.com/brad/copymyths.html

'Ten big myths about copyright explained', Brad Templeton. 'An attempt to answer common myths about copyright seen on the net and cover issues related to copyright and USENET/Internet publication.'

http://www.rbs2.com/plag.htm

'Plagiarism in Colleges in USA', Ronald B. Standler. This detailed discussion of the legal aspects of plagiarism is cited frequently and nearly always positively by lists like this. It includes references to legal cases and offers views on how universities should manage the difference between plagiarism and copyright.

Paper mills and cheat sites

There are literally hundreds of these sites and they change regularly. If you find one, it will link to many others. A good way to start is with a catalogue site such as:

http://www.coastal.edu/library/mills2.htm

Lists more than 150 'paper mills', including free sites and pay-per-page 'services'. It also categorises sites by topic and disciplines.

http://www.essaycrawler.com

Offers 35,000 free essays '… so you can get done and get on with your life'. This is also a good place to start if you suspect a student's paper has been purchased.

http://www.revise.it

Offers free essays on Economics, Philosophy, English Literature and Politics and is one of the earliest UK sites. It also offers guidance on how to make an essay look like something you wrote rather than plagiarised, advice that the site authors claim is 'a joke'.

http://www.study-area.com/student

Claims to be a site for UK students and offers 1200 documents for £5 per month or £15 per year . The free 'previews' appear very American.

Electronic detection

http://www.copycatch.freeserve.co.uk/vocalyse.htm

CopyCatch checks for collusion and copying between students.

http://www.turnitin.com/new.html

Turnitin.com offers an online service that checks the Web and builds a database of past submissions. Free trials are offered.

http://www.plagiarism.com/INDEX.HTM

The Glatt Detection site offers tools for self teaching and checking authorship. The site claims to be especially useful for authentication if the original source is not found.

http://www.canexus.com/eve/index.shtml

For a free trial download program of EVE or the Essay Verification Engine.

http://www.cs.berkeley.edu/~aiken/moss.html

MOSS or Measure of Software Similarity, often used with JPlag (below).

http://wwwipd.ira.uka.de:2222/

JPlag, useful in source code plagiarism detection.

Comments on exercises

In all cases, reflection, discussion and sharing of views is more important than 'the right answer'. For some, it is the only purpose. However, I offer below my experience of running these exercises in groups.

Page 18: Students' motivations for cheating

I believe the literature shows that reasons 5 and 1 (misunderstanding and last minute panic) are the most frequent for UK students. International students are more likely to be driven by reasons 4 and 6 (pressure to succeed and inability to do the work) than by 10 (cultural misunderstandings), especially if the plagiarism happens after the first term of work. However, reason 10 for not using a paraphrase is common for international students later in their course if the piece of work is very important, reinforcing reason 4. Reason 9 (misunderstanding collaboration and collusion) is common as a genuine reason in beginners for both UK and international students. Reason 7 (deliberate, planned fraud) is rare and in some cohorts, even nonexistent. Anecdotal evidence about deliberate cheating is more common than careful surveys but most academics worry that it is becoming more common. I often point out that general trends are not helpful with subgroups. For example, Whiteley and Keith-Spiegel (2002, p. 31) found a strong link between those who cheat and those who 'party a lot' so reasons 2 (not keeping up) and 8 (just needing to pass) are probably most common for this group. Of course, students claim reasons they think will strengthen their case for avoiding punishment so statistics may reflect this.

Page 42: Where do you draw the line?

Those who teach students with few writing skills often say, "2 is not acceptable but if I can get the students to 3, then I'm happy". Others state that 3 is not acceptable but 4 would be worth a mark because the student did some work, adding that they probably would not spot the lack of quotation marks anyway. When I do this exercise with students, they come up with many different answers, especially at induction sessions. When there is time, I ask if they can explain why the line must be drawn between numbers 4 and 5. Insisting that 4 is not acceptable with teaching staff whereas 5 is, often results in a discussion on the difference between the real and ideal and how best to work within this spectrum.

Page 52: Differentiating cheating behaviours

I use this exercise to check students' and lecturers' understanding of plagiarism. Groups of three or four can correct and inform each other without putting anyone on the spot. I sometimes finish the exercise by offering a diagram like that on the left, designed to show that plagiarism is a subset of cheating and collusion a subset of plagiarism. Most groups argue about where best to put numbers 14 and 15 and thereby usually clarify the meaning of concepts like "passing off work" and "doing your own work".

Cheating

Plagiarism

Collusion

Cheating	Plagiarism	Collusion
2	3	1
4	6	5
7	9	10
8	12	16
11	13	17
14*	14*	
15*	15*	

Bibliography

All web sites listed here were active in July 2002.

Angelil-Carter, S. (2000), 'Understanding plagiarism differently', in Leibowitz, B. and Mohammed, Y. (eds.), *Routes to Writing in Southern Africa* (Cape Town: Silk Road International Publishers)

Bannister, P. and Ashworth, P. (1998), 'Four good reasons for cheating and plagiarism', in Rust, C. (ed.), *Improving Student Learning Symposium*, (Oxford: Oxford Centre for Staff and Learning Development, Oxford Brookes University) pp. 233 241

Biggs, J. (1999), *Teaching for Quality Learning in Higher Education*, p. 129, quoting Wilson (1997) (Milton Keynes: Open University)

Bligh, D. (1998), *What's the Use of Lectures?* (Exeter: Intellect)

Boehm, D. (1998), 'Well-designed assignments: a third solution', http://www.svsu.edu/~dboehm/Assignments.htm

Bull, J., Collins, C., Coughlin, E. and Sharpe, D. (2001), 'Technical Review of Plagiarism Detection Software Report', http://www.jisc.ac.uk/pub01/luton.pdf

Carroll, J. and Appleton, J. (2001), 'Plagiarism: a good practice guide', http://www.jisc.ac.uk/pub01/brookes.pdf

Carroll, J. and Pepperell, H. (2002), 'The effects of electronic detection on student learning' (in press)

Chester, G. (2001), 'Plagiarism Detection, and Prevention: final report of the JISC electronic plagiarism detection project' http://www.jisc.ac.uk/pub01/plagiarism_final.pdf

Cole, S. and Kiss, E. (2000), 'What can we do about student cheating?', *About Campus*, May–June, 2000, pp. 5–12

Coverdale, J. and Henning, M. (2000), 'An analysis of cheating behaviour during training by medical students', *Medical Teacher* 22,6 pp. 582–584

Cox, A., Currall, J. and Connolly, S. (2001) 'The human and organisational issues associated with network security' http://litc.sbu.ac.uk/jcalt

Culwin, F. and Lancaster, T. (2001) 'Plagiarism prevention and detection' http://cise.sbu.ac.uk

Culwin, F., MacLeod, A. and Lancaster, T. (2001) 'Source code plagiarism in UK HE computing schools: issues, attitudes and tools' http://www.jisc.ac.uk/pub01/southbank.pdf

Davies, P. 'Computerised peer assessment and plagiarism: removing the tutor from the process' (in press)

Decoo, W. (2002), *Crisis on Campus: confronting academic misconduct* (Cambridge, Mass.: MIT Press)

Errey, L. 'Plagiarism: something fishy or a fish out of water?' (in press)

Evans, J. (2000), 'Autoplagiarism', *Educational Technology News*, Summer, p.12

Evans, J. (2000), 'The new plagiarism in Higher Education: from selection to reflection' http://www.warwick.ac.uk/ETS/interactions/vol4no2/evans.html

Fly, B., vanBark, W., Weinman, L., Kitchener, K., and Lang, P. (1997) 'Ethical transgressions of psychology graduate students', *Professional Psychology Research and Practice*, 28, 5, pp. 492–495

Fox, H. (1994), *Listening to the World: Cultural Issues in Academic Writing* (Urbana, Illinois: National Council of Teachers of English)

Franklyn-Stokes and Newstead (1995), 'Undergraduate cheating: who does what and why', *Studies in Higher Education*, 20:2 pp. 159–172

Freewood, M. (2001), 'Student perceptions of plagiarism: a research project' (Sheffield Hallam University Plagiarism and Inappropriate Collusion Steering Group)

Fritz, C., Morris, P., Bjork, R., Gelman, R., and Wickens, T. (2000) 'When learning fails: stability and change following repeated presentation of text', *British Journal of Psychology*, 91, 4, pp. 493–511

Furedi, F. (2000), 'Online cat and mouse', *Times Higher Education Supplement*, 14 July, 2000

Gajadhar, J. (1998), 'Issues in plagiarism for the new millennium: an assessment odyssey', http://ultibase.rmit.edu.au/Articles/dec98/gajad1.htm

Grossman, W. (2002), 'All their own work?',*The Independent*, 15 April, 2002

Hanlon, W. (2002), 'Sharpening students' analytical skills', in *Focus on university teaching and learning*, Dalhousie University, 11, 3

Harris, R. (2001) 'Anti-plagiarism strategies in research papers', http://www.virtualsalt.com/antiplag.htm

Harris, R. (2001), *The Plagiarism Handbook*, (Los Angeles: Pyrczak Publishing)

Hart, N. (2001), *Education Brief* 23, pp. 3–6 (Martineau Johnson)

Hinchliffe, L. (1998), 'Cut and paste plagiarism: preventing, detecting and tracking on line plagiarism' http://alexia.lis.uiuc.edu/~janicke/plagiary.htm

Hinchliffe, L. (2000), 'Can the computer identify plagiarism?' *The CATalyst*, February 5–6 (Centre for the Advancement of Teaching, Illinois State University)

JISC (Joint Information Systems Committee) (2001), Chester, G. 'Plagiarism Detection and Prevention: final report on the JISC electronic plagiarism detection project', http://www.jisc.ac.uk/pub01/plagiarism_final.pdf

Macdonald, R. (2000), 'Why don't we turn the tide of plagiarism to the learner's advantage?', *Times Higher Education Supplement*, 24 November, 2000

McCabe, D. (2002), 'CAI research', http://academicintegrity.org/cai_research.asp

McDowell, L. and Brown, S. (2001), 'Assessing students: cheating and plagiarism' on http://www.ilt.ac.uk (access to the paper restricted to members of ILT)

McKenzie, J. (1998), 'The new plagiarism: seven antidotes to prevent highway robbery in an electronic age', http://www.fno.org/may98/cov98may.html

McNaughton, W. (1995), *Student Handbook on Writing Research Papers* (Department of Chinese, Translation and Linguistics, City University of Hong Kong), cited on http://www.cityu.edu.hk/pdqs/rft/98-002.html

Mirow, M. and Shore, P. (1997), 'Plagiarism and textual ownership in the digital source environment', *Proteus: a journal of ideas* 14,1, pp. 41–43

Okkelmo, S. (2001), 'Other people's essays', in HERO, 3 January 2001 on http://www.hero.ac.uk/studying/archive/other_people_s_essays908.cfm

Olsen, V. (1998), 'Jane Eyre to go', *Salon Magazine* http://www.salon.com/it/career/1998/11/13career.html

Price, M., O'Donovan, B. and Rust, C. (2000) 'Strategies to develop students' understanding of assessment criteria and processes', in Rust, C. (ed.), *Improving Student Learning Symposium* (Oxford: Oxford Centre for Staff and Learning Development, Oxford Brookes University)

Quality Assurance Agency (2000), *Quality and Standards in HE – Assessment of Students*

Roig, M. and deTommaso, L. (1995), 'Are college cheating and plagiarism related to academic procrastination?' *Psychological Reports* 77, 691–698

Rust, C. (2001), 'A briefing on assessment of large groups' in LTSN Generic Centre Assessment Series, 12
http://www.ltsn.ac.uk/genericcentre/projects/assessment/assess_series/12LargeGroups.pdf

Ryan, J. (2000), *A Guide to Teaching International Students* (Oxford: Oxford Centre for Staff and Learning Development, Oxford Brookes University)

Standler, R. (2000), 'Plagiarism in Colleges in the USA'
http://www.rbs2.com/plag.htm

Stevens, J. (2002), 'On plagiarism and performance', *ILT Newsletter*, 8,Spring, 4

Swales, J. and Feak, C. (1994), *Academic Writing for Graduate Students*, (AnnArbour: University of Michigan)

Volet, S. and Kee, J. (1993), 'Studying in Singapore – studying in Australia', Murdoch University Teaching Excellence Series – Occasional paper 1

Wahrer, S. (2002), 'Plagiarism: avoiding the greatest academic sin',
http://www.bgsu.edu/offices/acen/writerslab/handouts/plagiarism.pdf

Walker, J. (1998), 'Student plagiarism in universities: what are we doing about it?', *Higher Education Research and Development* 17, 1, 89–106

Watkins, J. and Biggs, J. (1996), *The Chinese Learner* (Hong Kong: Comparative Education Research Centre)

Weeks, S. (2001), 'Think before pointing the finger of blame', *Times Higher Education Supplement*, 18 May 2001 p. 24

Whitely, B. and Keith-Spiegel, P. (2002), *Academic Dishonesty: An Educator's Guide*, (Lawrence Erlbaum Associates)

Wilhoit, S. (1994), 'Helping students avoid plagiarism', *College Teaching* 42,4, pp.161–164

Wilson, K. (1997) 'Wording it up: plagiarism and the interdiscourse of international students', paper given to the annual conference, Higher Education Research and Development Society of Australia, Adelaide, 8–11 July